Dinosaurs to Rabbits:
Turning Mainline Decline to a Multiplication Movement

Bill Easum
Bill Tenny-Brittian

ISBN: 1718653700
ISBN-13: 978-1718653702

ENDORSEMENTS

Ironically, most mainline denominations began as movements, but along the way drifted and became monuments. Bill and Bill point us back to lead us forward. They remind us mainliners that generative growth is not only possible but is our birthright as the church and is really happening today. This is a simple yet profound prophetic book that will not only challenge you, but help you take next steps to join Jesus in his mission in the world.

Jorge Acevedo
Lead Pastor
Grace Church
A Multi-Site United Methodist congregation

Many of the mainline churches in North America were once multiplication movements. With years of wisdom and practical experience, Bill Easum and Bill Tenny-Brittian are prophetic voices calling mainline churches back to the foundation of church multiplication. If you want to unleash a disciple making movement within your denominational context, I highly recommend this book!

Dr. Winfield Bevins
Director of Church Planting
Asbury Seminary
Author of *Marks of a Movement*

Dinosaurs to Rabbits is not a fluffy soft read, but a hard-hitting exposition toward turning declining mainline congregations into a multiplication movement. Easum and Tenny-Brittian have done it again. This book is one worth wrestling over. It will encourage you one moment and get your irritation up the next. Get over it and step up to ponder these great lessons and truths. You will not want to gloss over chapters 3 (A Theology of Growth) and 4 (Radical Discipleship). There is great wisdom and incredible power within these two sections alone. In a day where much grey is found in the church world, these men will draw you back to the principles of multiplication. They provide ten critical ripples regarding multiplication that every church ought to have placed in their conference rooms. Walk amidst this work, wrestle with your discomfort, then witness to others regarding the power of transformation for multiplication this book has had on your life. You won't regret it.

Tom Cheyney
Founder & Directional Leader
The Renovate National Church Revitalization Conference
Author of *Slaying the Dragons of Church Revitalization*

Years ago I was in a meeting with one hundred young pastors all of whom were growing their churches at a rapid rate. I was the only mainline guy at the meeting. One of Bill Easum's books was the discussion topic. During a break, one of the young pastors came to me and asked, " Since Bill Easum is a member of your tribe, why don't you guys listen to him?" I could not answer the question.

With this outstanding book, Bill Easum and Bill Tenny-Brittian have once again spoken truth to the mainline. This may be the most needed book yet. We would do well to listen to them this time.

J. Clif Christopher
President - Founder
Horizons Stewardship Co.
Author of *Not Your Parents' Offering Plate*

Don't read this book ... unless you're willing to be stretched, unless you want to become more passionate about reaching the lost, unless you're willing to raise up lay leaders who might outshine you, and unless you're willing for the church you lead to look more like the good stuff that happened in the Book of Acts. This is a book by mainliners for mainliners, so it speaks to your world. I dare you to take the risk of buying several copies and reading it with a group of leaders and potential leaders from your church.

Warren Bird, Ph.D.
Co-author of 30 books for church leaders including *Hero Maker: Five Essential Practices for Leaders to Multiply Leaders*

Forged in the fire of conviction, Easum and Tenny-Brittian have hammered into shape a powerful and potent plow capable of breaking-up the fallow ground of today's Mainline church in their new book *From Dinosaurs to Rabbits*. With careful application of scripture, penetrating insights from decades of fruitful consulting, and proven pastoral ministry, the authors convince and then invite every church member of every kind to put their hand to that plow and join them in the harvest. This prophetic little book may anger its readers; it may get lambasted on social media; and tragically ignored by those who most should read it. But for those audacious enough to believe that Almighty God has a better future for His church than the one currently being experienced, to those hungry enough to see their communities transformed by Jesus Christ, and those wearied by the excuses of what cannot be done about the state of the church – if they dare read this book, their world will never be the same.

Tom Clegg
Senior Partner
The Clegg Consulting Group

Dancing with Dinosaurs was a revolutionary book for me in 1993. It offered new paradigms for ministry and confirmed what I was feeling and experiencing as a pastor. Here we are today, 2018, facing more paradigm shifts in our post-Christian world. *Dinosaurs to Rabbits* is a must read for those who want and dream of a fruitful future as a mainline church in America. Multiplication is one of the ways of the future in our ever changing, complex world. Learning how to move from addition-based growth to multiplication growth is key for the church to reach new people fast enough to replace the saints who are aging out.

Bishop Bob Farr
Missouri Conference of The United Methodist Church

If you accept the challenge in *Dinosaurs to Rabbits: Turning Mainline Decline to a Multiplication Movement*, you just might change your church, your denomination, and even the world. This is a must read for every mainline denominational church that wants to grow and multiply.

Dave Ferguson
Lead Pastor
Community Christian Church
Author of *Hero Maker: Five Essential Practices for Leaders to Multiply Leaders*

I love this book! Easum and Tenny-Brittian offer readers a game changing book in *Dinosaurs and Rabbits*. Understanding they are shaking the framework of mainline churches, they press on offering inspiration, encouragement, and many practical tools to shift from survival to multiplying church culture and strategy! May courageous leaders with deep faith and commitment step up now!

Edward Hammett
Author of *Reaching People Under 30 While Keeping People Over 60*

Provocative, challenging, and deeply insightful; this book is saturated with concrete practical recommendations that can readily be put into a practice by a pastor with a heart for the Great Commission. If you're tired of leading a slowly dying church then *Dinosaurs to Rabbits* is for you!

Bishop Mike Lowry
Resident Bishop of The Central Texas Conference of the United Methodist Church

It is widely reported that Mark Twain once said, "Everybody talks about the weather, but nobody does anything about it." The same could be said about the decline of the mainline churches over the last half century in the USA. While many observers have talked about mainline decline, few have offered any real thoughts on how to reverse it, that is, until now. In *Dinosaurs to Rabbits: Turning Mainline Decline into a Multiplication Movement*, Bill Easum and Bill Tenny-Brittian offer insightful perspectives on this important issue. Building on their experience as successful pastors in North America's mainline denominations, they add years of fruitful ministry as church consultants to provide a radical and doable approach for turnaround among America's mainline churches. Believe me, it's worth your time to read it. Even more, it's worth your time to put their ideas into action.

Gary L. McIntosh, D.Min., Ph.D.
Professor, Writer, and Speaker
Talbot School of Theology, La Mirada, CA

I do a lot of work with leaders of mainline denominations. A lot of it is grief therapy. It doesn't have to be this way. In *Dinosaurs to Rabbits*, the authors give practical, grounded, proven suggestions for church leaders who want to shift their church culture from church-as-institution to church-as-movement. This book nails it – from diagnosis to prescription. Nothing less than creating Jesus-followers who view and lead their lives as a mission trip will give mainlines a shot to move beyond paleontology.

Reggie McNeal
Speaker, Consultant and Best-Selling Author, *Kingdom Come and Kingdom Conspiracy*

Having first met Jesus in a mainline "dinosaur church," I am thankful for their faithfulness. Having also spent my life multiplying autonomous congregations, I believe the future hope of mainline churches is found in the pages of this book. If you are interested, you can multiply "rabbits" by following the trails outlined by Easum and Tenny-Brittian. Our culture awaits you.

Ralph Moore
Founder
Hope Chapel churches

Whether your church is mega, mini or multi, denom or nondenon, mainline, oldline, sideline or offline, you need this book to keep from flatlining. The future belongs to those with the best algorithms, and Easum and Tenny-Brittian probe the algorithms of the Spirit which are not addition or division but multiplication and incarnation.

Leonard Sweet
Professor: Drew University, Evangelical Seminary,
Tabor College, Portland Seminary
Author of 60 plus books, and founder/chief contributor to preachthestory.com

WARNING

What you are about to read might upset, offend or downright anger you. But please keep two things in mind as you read: One, we have been Mainline pastors for more than fifty years and still are; and Two, we only have one prayer for Mainline Christianity – that it will regain its former glory.

Bill Easum
Bill Tenny-Brittian

CONTENTS

1
WHY MULTIPLICATION?

"If you can see the harvest, you can take the risk."
Bill Easum

Learning how to multiply everything we do is the only hope for Mainline Christianity to regain the West. We are losing ground so fast, if something radical isn't done soon we will soon become an irrelevant part of the West's distant past. Relying on adding a few people here and there won't come close to replacing the thousands of people we are losing daily. Meanwhile the population continues to grow.

In the following pages, Mainline Christians will find a formula for the multiplication of every aspect of our ministry. Instead of slowly growing or dying by addition, you will learn to rapidly grow your church and the kingdom by thinking and acting multiplication. You will be encouraged to make multiplication an attitude that pervades everything your church or denomination does. What if Mainliners, pastors and laity, began to think multiplication instead of settling for addition, conflict, decline, and death? I believe it is the only hope for Western Christianity.

The Beginning Story

I was sitting in a room with fifteen of the key leaders of Western Christianity listening to the most mind blogging conversations I had ever heard. These leaders were telling stories about churches that had planted dozens of churches over the past twenty years. One church was telling stories from the 2500 churches they had either planted or had been planted by the churches they had planted. Another pastor told of a ten-year old church that had already planted more than fifty churches. Yet another leader told of sending twenty members across the Pacific to plant a church. And the kicker was, every one of these churches had grown despite giving hundreds of people away to plant churches (this isn't a book about church planting).

The stories went on and on and no one in the group seemed surprised by the stories – except me. In fact, not only were they not surprised, they were determined to multiply the number of churches experiencing such success. It didn't take long for me to see the harvest that could come from this kind of mindset.[1]

Turns out, I was the only Mainline leader in the room and I felt like I was representing a dinosaur. Everyone else was from an autonomous and conservative tribe. I wondered at the time why I'd been invited. I knew my reputation as a consultant was good, but I had limited experience with anything close to what was happening in these stories. Their invitation made no sense to me at the time, but after several of these sessions it became clear. God had put me there so I could go home and communicate with my Mainline colleagues the harvest that can come from growing by multiplication rather than by addition or subtraction.

But what would multiplication look like for Mainliners? That is the subject of this book.

The Multiplication Movement

There is a rapidly expanding movement in Christianity that, for the moment, is bypassing most of my Mainline colleagues. It's a movement so powerful it could change the trajectory of Christianity and win the West back from secularism. It's a movement I believe that Mainline leaders need to take stock of and join. I call it the multiplication movement.[2] The leaders of this movement are dedicated to multiplying everything from leaders to churches. The more I'm around them, the more I am convinced their type of passion is the future of Western Christianity.

For the last couple of years, I've spent a lot of time with these leaders. We've strategized and dreamed about how to refine and expand this movement. In one of these strategy sessions I remember thinking, "I would give anything for my Mainline friends to be part of these conversations and catch a glimpse of this harvest and what it would mean for the kingdom. But it can only happen if they focus on multiplication instead of survival or mere addition." But for now, this harvest of multiplication is either a mystery or an unknown to most Mainline pastors and denominational leaders. Most are simply trying to survive, we're dinosaurs in the midst of the ice age. Sure,

---

[1] From this experience Bill Tenny-Brittian and I wrote the book *From Scarcity to Abundance: Creating a Culture of Multiplication*. You can get it free at Exponential.org

[2] Exponential is the founder and main promoter of this movement. See www.exponential.org

there are a few growing Mainline churches that are adding a few people here and there, and there are an even smaller number that are focusing on reproduction, most often through Multi-Sites or a few church plants. But the gap between Mainline leaders and the harvest of multiplication remains wider than the Grand Canyon.

My most profound hope is that Mainline Christianity will see the genius and the potential harvest of multiplication and join the movement.

The Harvest

To join the multiplication movement, Mainline pastors and denominational officials will need to reorient many of their priorities, such as:

- We must become more passionate about redeeming the lost;
- We must put less emphasis on ordained clergy and more on the priesthood of believer;
- We must value discipleship more than membership;
- We must promote hands-on ministry more than committee work;
- We must commit to transformation over education;
- We must embrace the power of transformational small groups;
- We must surrender centralized control for the sake of more spontaneous, Spirit led freedom.
- We must seek out the mavericks on the fringes and learn from them.

Of course, making any change in an existing church involves risk. For instance:

- If we become passionate about reaching the lost, we risk alienating longstanding church members who don't appreciate not being the church's priority.
- If we emphasize the priesthood of the believer over ordination, we risk losing control of the church's programming and ministries.
- If we value discipleship over membership, we risk losing our consumer-committed members.
- If we promote hand's on ministry more than committee work, we risk not getting important "church work" done.
- If we commit to transformation over education, we risk turning our backs on the lectionary, packaged curriculum, small group book studies and even our seminaries.
- If we embrace the power of transformational groups, we risk raising the ire of our Sunday school classes as we shut them down.
- If we surrender centralized control for the sake of Spirit-led spontaneity, we risk uncontrollable chaos.
- If we seek out and learn from the mavericks, we risk having to admit

3

our leadership has been largely responsible for the decline of our churches.

Any change involves a risk, but the risk is worth it if we see it in view of the harvest. Just think what it would mean to your church if instead of having one adult baptism next year you have two and then four and then sixteen. Or instead of having one or two small groups, the number multiplies every eighteen months. Or instead of planting one church next year, you plant five churches and then fifteen. Or instead of acquiescing to bullies who try to control the congregation, faithful disciples push back to the point the bullies step aside or leave. I could go on, but surely you can glimpse the harvest – it's multiples of new Christians over and over, enough to win back the West in the next few decades!

The Book of Acts gives us a snapshot of this harvest.

- The harvest started small with a handful of carefully chosen followers who were mentored for three years before the harvest began in earnest.
- Acts 1 and 2 tell us that the early church went from 120 believers to 3,120 believers overnight.
- Acts 2:47 says, "Each day the Lord added to their group those who were being saved." The number of Christians was growing daily!
- Acts 5:28 says, "You have filled all Jerusalem with your teaching about Jesus."
- Acts 6:1 says, "The believers rapidly multiplied." It is only now, after all this growth, that they use the word "rapidly."
- "Acts 6:7 says, "So the word of God increased, and the number of disciples in Jerusalem **multiplied**."
- In Acts 9:31, "Therefore, the church throughout the whole of Judea, Galilee, and Samaria had peace, being built up and walking in the fear of the Lord and in the encouragement of the Holy Spirit it was **multiplying**."
- But this wildfire of growth was not over. Acts 21:20 uses another word for this harvest – *murias,* from which we get the word myriad. The word means tens of thousands … there were literally tens of thousands of believers in Jerusalem by the time Paul was arrested in Jerusalem.

It's clear from this brief snapshot that the author of Acts is telling us that Christianity didn't grow by addition; it grew by multiplication!

Donald McGavran, the father of the Church Growth Movement, once asked, "What is the true fruit of an apple tree?" The response was, "It's an apple, of course." Then McGavran rebutted, "You're wrong. The true fruit of an apple tree is not an apple, but another apple tree."

My friends, if you can imagine this beautiful harvest, you can take the risk and join the multiplication movement.

To understand the powerful impact of multiplication we need to look at the difference between focusing on addition and focusing on multiplication. That's the subject of the next chapter.

2
ADDITION OR MULITIPLICATION?

As we know, most Mainline congregations are rapidly shrinking. Some are holding on only because of their endowments given by generous members of the past. Others are scraping by, hoping for a miracle. And a few, some suggest less than 20 percent, are growing.[3] Most of those that are growing are growing slowly by addition. In fact, it's estimated that less than 4 percent of all churches in the US are growing at a reproducible rate.[4] Churches growing by addition are adding more people each year than they are losing. However, the hidden factor in this growth by addition is that the average age of these congregations is getting older each year, which means that no matter how much they grow by addition, it's only a matter of time for most of these congregations because they will age out, unless something changes. That something is growth by multiplication.

The difference between church multiplication and addition can best be described by a comparison of dinosaurs to rabbits. By and large, dinosaurs weren't created with multiplication in mind, especially not the larger ones most of us are familiar with like the tyrannosaurus rex, brachiosaurus, stegosaurus, and triceratops. These dinosaurs laid from three to twenty-one eggs in each clutch. That sounds promising; however, most of the eggs in the nest were quickly devoured by predators. And since it took between six to nine months for an egg to hatch, few eggs in a clutch survived. Of those that did survive, only the fittest and fastest hatchlings escaped being gobbled up by one carnivore or another once they were free of the egg. On average, it's likely only one hatchling in a clutch survived the birth process and some

---

[3] Todd Wilson, et al, *Becoming a Level Five Church Field Guide* (Exponential.org, 2015), 33.
[4] Ibid.

scientists have suggested this is one of the reasons for the prehistoric extinctions.

When it comes to church growth in the Mainline, we've been laying a lot of eggs. We've acted as if Pack-A-Pew Sundays, ecumenical food pantries, and replacing the communion hymn with a praise chorus is going to launch a revival and the wayward will begin pouring in. I still see pastors pounding on the pulpits telling their members *they* need to invite their friends … but they themselves don't have a single unchurched, unbelieving friend. And we still get pushback whenever we suggest that organ music, classic choirs, and clergy robes are more effective in a museum than a growing church.

Too many Mainline denominations still cling to the notion that the community would somehow be poorer if *their* brand of Christianity went missing – without understanding that virtually no one in the neighborhood would even notice if they closed up shop and quietly went home.

The need to bring our Mainline flavor of the month continues to influence what we believe about starting new churches. Too many of us still think the way of the future is to start new churches by buying land, constructing a building, hiring a thirty-something seminary-trained pastor, and putting up a sign that says, *Everyone Welcome*. Ahh, if only they had the money!

We're like the dinosaurs that keep laying eggs. Most of our plans never see the light of the day. Mainline churches are notorious for talking about what needs to be done, studying what could be done, assigning a committee to explore possibilities, turning to the finance committee to weigh out the costs, and ultimately seeing the plans fade into oblivion as time inevitably passes by the opportunity. But now and again, an egg *will* hatch and we'll see another ministry launch, another leader rise up, a second site or a new church launched. But all around us, dinosaur after dinosaur falls into the tar pits of tradition and entropy and there just aren't enough baby dinosaurs being born to keep up, let alone get ahead. Too soon, like the dancing dinosaurs before the ice age, we'll become extinct. Winter's coming.

On the other hand, rabbits appear to have been created with multiplication in their genes. Whereas, dinosaurs generally managed to produce one infant per nest, rabbits have about six baby bunnies with each kit. The gestation period for a rabbit is thirty-one days, and the female is fertile hours after birth. Whereas a dinosaur may have one or two living hatchlings in a year, a rabbit has over seventy per year … and the new bunnies begin breeding by the time they're six months. That means within a year of a female's first litter, there will be over 700 bunnies hopping around, with each one clamoring to reproduce again. And again.

Dinosaurs are extinct; rabbits are everywhere. Rabbits are designed to multiply; it's in their DNA. For Mainline congregations to return to their former glory we must think and act like rabbits. We must multiply; we cannot afford to just add.

It will help us understand multiplication and the difficulties involved in Mainline congregations growing by multiplication if we explore the specific differences between addition and multiplication. These differences are far more than the difference between the numbers one and two.

To begin, take a quick look at the following comparisons. And please, as you read the rest of this section, don't get offended; the following comparisons come from Mainliners who've been where you are today.

Addition	Multiplication
Number of people in worship	Number of people given away
Formal Seminary Training	Local church training
Buildings	Anywhere
Expensive	Inexpensive
Come	Go
Church	Kingdom
Curriculum/Programs	Relationships
Hire from without	Call from within
Personal piety	World revolution
Consumers	Servants
Nominal	Radical
Regulations	Spontaneous Freedom

Most Mainline churches focus on their members and on attracting new members. "Come join us" is their mantra. If they are successful, they must invest most of their dollars in buildings and paid staff. The result being they come to revere their buildings, treat their members as consumers whose wishes must be met, and believe that keeping their congregation alive and their church's "open" is the primary goal. If they do anything beyond their church, it is give money to some foreign mission or food pantry that has little or no impact on their future.

However ...

Churches focused on multiplication score their effectiveness by how many disciples they can raise up and give away to serve others in the community. "Go and serve" is their mantra. Radical discipleship replaces nominal membership. And while a healthy worship attendance is important, it's not the goal. Rather than focusing on attracting new people, these churches focus on how many disciples they can send out into the community or world. Serving is more important than the congregation becoming big and the kingdom is more important than their congregation. If a new church moves into their community they celebrate because it will benefit the kingdom.

On the Other Hand …

Most Mainline churches focus on providing programs for their members. In many cases these programs have little to do with either making disciples or growing the kingdom. These programs take money and people to run them. The more programs a church has, the less time the members can spend in the community sharing Christ.

However …

Churches focused on multiplication understand that relationships are more important than programs. Rather than having a variety of programs they focus primarily on transformational small groups that meet in homes and whose primary goal is to disciple and raise up the future leaders and servants who are willing to be sent into the community to serve. Small groups are far less expensive than most programs, which leave more money for outreach.

On the Other Hand …

Most Mainline churches give more credibility to academic credentials than they do to demonstrated credentials, so they require their clergy to have seminary training. Almost every job description for a Mainline clergy has academic achievements at the top of the list of requirements. The problem with this is two-fold: (1) Seminaries admit it's not their responsibility to turn out leaders; and (2) Today's serious young disciples are too eager to be in full time ministry to spend three or more years in postgraduate studies when they can learn everything they need to make disciples by working in a multiplying local church.

However …

Churches focused on multiplication see every parishioner as someone willing to serve and be sent. They could serve as a potential pastor, small group leader, campus pastor, or church planter. So, most of these churches raise up their pastors and paid staff from within the membership. They can do this because they don't settle for nominal members. Instead, they provide the examples, mentors, and training required for both leadership and spiritual development. They provide the equivalent of an in-house, on-the-job seminary degree.

On the Other Hand …

Most Mainline churches see every parishioner as a potential resource for maintaining the local church. They count on retaining their members to ensure the church's sustainability. The notion of "sending out" their members to start a new church is counter-intuitive at best and terrifying at worst. And so they do everything they can do to hang on to their members, which means they emphasize harmony over accountability. Without accountability, members are pretty much free to believe whatever they want and to behave however they want, which means the church doesn't just tolerate nominal members, they produce them in abundance.

Jerusalem Versus Antioch

Another way to contrast the Mainlines' problem is to compare what happened in the Jerusalem church to the Antioch church. The Jerusalem church, like most Mainline churches, settled down in survival mode and focused on taking care of its own.[5] Even when most Christians fled from persecution, the Apostles remained in Jerusalem[6] and, over time, the church weakened to the point that financial assistance was necessary.[7] On the other hand, the Antioch church multiplied itself by sending out groups of missionaries to spread the word and plant churches. The church exists today, not because of the ministry of the Jerusalem church, but because of the sending capacity of the Antioch church.

Now you see why I asked you not to get offended. These comparisons are tough, but they go to the heart of what's robing Mainline Christianity of its soul, and its power. If Mainline Christianity is going to turn around and once again become a relevant force in the West we are going to have to shift gears from addition and attraction, to multiplication and sending. Failure to make this shift will result in the death of Mainline Christianity.

The Way Forward

The primary change Mainline churches must make if they want to shift from decline and addition to growth and multiplication is to allow the Great Commission to color everything they do. Jesus said "go," not "come." Jesus tried to focus our attention on others not ourselves. His last will and testament was a "send" command. We are sent people. We weren't meant to hunker down in our church buildings safe from the world. We were meant to be sent into the world with a message of redemption and new life.

---

[5] Acts 6
[6] Acts 8
[7] Acts 11

Anything less is apostasy. To put it bluntly, Mainline Christianity needs to recover a theology of growth and that is the subject of the next chapter.

3
A THEOLOGY OF GROWTH

"You can care for people without transforming them,
but you can't transform them without caring for them"
Bill Easum

(Warning: The madder this chapter makes you, the more reasons you must read it carefully and not make a knee jerk reaction.)

I think you would agree that what we believe determines what we do. Or to put it another way, our theology determines our actions. And what I've discovered over thirty years of working with thousands of pastors is the that the one thing separating ineffective pastors from effective pastors is what I call a "Theology of Growth."

A "Theology of Growth" is a deep-seated belief, both in personal salvation and kingdom growth. Effective pastors believe that all Christians should do their part in spreading the Good News. They believe the goal of every congregation is to baptize people, promote justice, and grow the kingdom. This belief means that being a nice, good person is never enough. Everyone needs to have Jesus as his or her Lord and when that happens the kingdom grows on earth. As the Scriptures say: *"For this reason also, God highly exalted him, and bestowed on him the name which is above every name, so that at the name of Jesus every knee will bow, of those who are in heaven and on earth and under the earth, and that every tongue will confess that Jesus Christ is Lord, to the glory of God the Father."*[8]

A "Theology of Growth" puts personal salvation, living justly, and the growth of the kingdom of God before all else. It insists that telling people

---

[8] Philippians 2:9–11

about Christ and bringing salvation to the world is the primary goal of Christianity. Everything else pales in comparison to this belief. Everything begins and ends with personal redemption. The lack of this passion and this commitment is the bane of Western Christianity!

The primary reason the Acts of the Apostles was written was to showcase a "Theology of Growth." Acts is far more than a history of the early church. It is an example of why God gave us the church. One cannot read the text without being struck by its constant reference to the growth of Christianity across most of the known world. Everything from the day of Pentecost when 3000 converts were added to the church, to the multiplication of churches everywhere the apostles traveled, spreading the word about Jesus was paramount. Earlier in the introduction, we saw how Acts recorded the progression of this growth and in doing so it introduced us to the "Theology of Growth."

Reaching the one lost sheep or coin or son is the heart of God.[9] It is why God gave us Jesus. As the scripture says: "For God so loved the world that God gave us the Son so that whoever believed in him would not perish but have everlasting life."[10] Sharing Jesus with the world is what fuels every effective pastor and church in the world. And the lack of this passion is at the heart of the Mainline problem.

The Heart of the Mainline Problem

Most Mainline Protestants have replaced a "Theology of Growth" with a "Theology of Life." We focus on the Great Commandment almost to the exclusion of the Great Commission. Instead of a deep-seated belief in sharing Jesus with the world, too many pastors believe that Christianity is primarily a way of life. For them, being good replaces sharing Jesus, and social justice replaces personal salvation. Many see their primary role to be that of a pastoral counselor. I've even had Mainline pastors make fun of me when I say the role of the pastor is to lead.

Many Mainline pastors act as if getting members to faithfully attend worship is their primary goal. Many are content if their worship attendance isn't declining. But Christianity isn't merely about faithfully attending worship or about being good. Many church members live good clean lives, love their neighbor, never break a law, support great charities, but never spread the Good News. This kind of faithfulness isn't what Christ died for. He died for much more. He died to save the world and he wants us to do our part. I'm not discounting faithfulness in doing good, but I am highlighting the need

---

[9] Luke 15

[10] John 3:16

for effectiveness when it comes to spreading the Gospel. It's one thing to be faithful; it's another to effectively spread the Good News. God needs Christians who faithfully and effectively share Jesus with their networks.

Mainline liberalism has perpetuated a Theology of Life that has drained the soul out of Mainline Christianity.

I see this Theology of Life acted out when:

- Pastors tell me, "All you are concerned about is numbers." Usually this means those pastors are leading dying congregations and don't want to own up to the fact that their actions aren't resulting in the growth of their churches, let alone Christianity. Worse yet, these pastors may be deluding themselves into believing that they are being faithful when all they are achieving is the care and feeding of spiritual infants who will never achieve God's potential for their lives.

- Pastors tell me that God called them to be caregivers instead of transformers. They feel their primary ministry is to be a chaplain and in extreme cases "assist their church to die." Where in God's name do you see such a role in the Scriptures? Pastors were never meant to be caregivers. They were meant to equip the church for the various ministry functions.[11] Pastors who see their primary role to be the care and feeding of the congregation need to step out of the role of pastor, take a staff position, and let someone whose primary task is to equip people to spread the Good News take their place. Caring for people isn't the goal of Christianity. Remember, I asked you not to get mad.

Sure, people need to be cared for, but they mostly need to be introduced to Jesus. And here's the kicker – you can care for people without transforming them; but you can't transform them without caring for them. But the goal is never care, it's transformation.

- Pastors make the pursuit of social justice their main ministry. I'm not making a case against social justice. Lord knows, I've spent a big part of my ministry fighting for the forgotten. But as important as social justice is, it doesn't hold a candle to personal salvation. The primarily goal of Christianity is always the spiritual transformation of everything, both personal and corporate.

- Church members won't stand up to those members who try to bully the congregation into doing only what *they* want done. They believe that being nice and being a Christian are one in the same. They

---

[11] See Ephesians 4:11–12

believe that civility is more important than growing the kingdom.[12] In my experience, most churches will grow if you eliminate one or two members who are against anything that doesn't benefit them.

- Churches fight over their turf when another church is planted in the area. Instead of rejoicing over their being more chances of reaching the unreached, the leaders hunker down and resist the new church. But when the growth of the kingdom becomes more important than the survival of one's church, then multiplication is possible.

A Theology of Growth

Acts 1:8 is a prime example of a Theology of Growth. "But you will receive power when the Holy Spirit comes on you; and you will be my witnesses in Jerusalem, and in all Judea and Samaria, and to the ends of the earth." Jesus told his disciples that the purpose of the Holy Spirit was to empower them to be his witness in all the world. And, as we saw in Chapter One, this theology leads to the multiplication of the faith.

So, what does a Theology of Growth involve?

For Mainline pastors to take part in the multiplication movement they must have a greater passion for the Great Commission than I normally see. One of the drivers of the multiplication movement is a deep-seated concern for lost people. But herein lies one of the greatest barriers for many Mainline pastors – their heart isn't broken over lost humanity. In fact, some of them don't believe that humanity is lost, with or without Jesus. Christianity is merely a way of life that serves the greater good – an ethical philosophy for life. This belief is a huge obstacle for most Mainline pastors.

Look at the following continuum and put an X at the spot that best describes your belief.

There are Multiple Ways to God   Jesus is the Only Way to God

Where you stand on this continuum will ultimately determine whether you have any chance of joining the multiplication movement. The closer you are to "Jesus is the Only Way" the more likely you are to have a broken heart over people who don't know Jesus, whereas the closer you are to "multiple ways" the less likely you are to even get involved in reaching out to the lost. Those on the far left often respond negatively even to the use of the word "lost" while those on the far right must be careful not to come off as a bigot. Those in the middle will have to work on being more urgent and passionate about their sharing the faith.

Now I know I'm on tricky ground here. The scandal of particularity has

[12] see Appendix A for more explanation

been debated for close to a hundred years. But this issue is at the heart of why Mainline Christianity is declining to the point that it is almost irrelevant to our world. Our society is becoming so secular that a "Theology of Good," where people are basically good and Christianity merely a way of life, doesn't mean squat anymore. Our secular society is past the belief that "God is on his throne and all is right with the world." The Great Society of the twentieth century has proven to be a failure and people are lost and in need of salvation.

Those who want to participate in the multiplication movement and change the world must be willing to say, "Jesus is Lord" and mean it. We must realize that without Jesus faith is little more than words. Every multiplication pastor I've met is convinced there is no room for doubting that Jesus is the *only* way to God.

I can't leave this section without sharing an experience I had with a pastor in the Northeast. I had spent three days at his church conducting a Ministry Audit.[13] When I finished the pastor drove me to the airport. Just as we arrived and I was about to exit the car, he said, "Several times this weekend you mentioned the need for a personal relationship with Jesus. What did you mean by that?" It's that misunderstanding of Jesus that is killing Mainline Christianity.

Before You Blow Me Off …

I know some of you are about to throw this book in the trash. What I've just said is so offensive to you that you are about to throw up. I hear you and I understand. But before you blow me off, hear me out. This issue is too crucial for you to give up on me. So, here is my question to you. If you are far to the left on the above continuum what difference is there between your ministry and that of the Lions Club? You're about doing good and so is the Lions Club. They are about helping people see better and so are you. You want to make a difference in the world but so do they. So, what's the difference? Of course, I could take this question to the next level and ask, what's the difference between your church and a Mosque? What do you have to offer that they don't have? These are crucial questions that we must ask and answer if we want to participate in the multiplication movement.

Now, if you're still with me, let's not let those on the far right off without asking them some tough questions. Are you able to share Jesus without coming off like a bigot? Are you sure you aren't taking a position of superiority? Are you willing to start the conversation where *they* are rather than where you are? Are you willing to listen before you speak?

Whatever else we can say about a Theology of Growth we must never see Christianity as some egalitarian faith. It's not "we're better than you." Instead,

---

[13] You can purchase a copy of The Ministry Audit by going to our store at https://effectivechurch.net/store/complete-ministry-audit-digital-edition/

it's "we have something that will enrich your life." So, a Theology of Growth is premised on the belief in the ultimate value of every human being. Jesus is not something to be lauded over others. Jesus is the fulfillment of our DNA!

In short, the theology of Growth, has its roots in the Great Commission and its fulfillment in radical discipleship. The next chapter is devoted to making the kind of disciples who can change the world and win back the West to Christianity.

4

RADICAL DISCIPLESHIP

"He indeed bears fruit and yields,
in one case a hundredfold,
in another sixty, and in another thirty."
Matthew 13:23

The primary ingredient in multiplication is radical discipleship. Radical discipleship goes beyond the accepted norm to where every facet of a person's life is shaped by the gospel. It's more than attending a membership class, or worship, or even being a tither. It's about walking and talking and acting like Jesus. Radical discipleship is of such a nature that if we even come close to it in our daily lives others will want to know what we have that they don't have, which opens the door for us to share our faith. This kind of radical discipleship leads to multiplication.

The Problem

Mainline churches haven't seen many radical disciples over the past six or seven decades. Most of our churches are full of nominal Christians who act more like consumers than servants. They treat their pastor as a hired servant rather than their leader.

We've seen decades of church consumers, shopping for the church that meets their need. It is now so bad in the U.S. that most pastors are delighted if their parishioners simply show up. That kind of discipleship won't cut it. A radical disciple doesn't have to be encouraged to show up on Sunday morning or become involved in mission projects, or share their faith with their neighbors – they just do it because that's who they are. They are radical about their faith and you know them when you see them.

The Word "Disciple" Doesn't Mean Much Anymore

The word disciple is so watered down that it means little more than being a church member who shows up on a fairly regular basis and goes to meetings. But that's not the kind of discipleship that will fuel a multiplication movement. So, we need to drill down on the biblical meaning of the word disciple.

Using today's definitions and understandings, a more accurate word for "disciple" is "apprentice." Apprentices spend most of their time hanging out with a master craftsman learning a trade by hands-on-learning. They don't study about what it means to be an apprentice, instead they simply do what the master is doing. And as they do, they get better and better until you can't tell them from the master craftsman. Discipleship isn't something that can be learned in a classroom. It's something that's caught rather than taught.

However, most of the disciple making that occurs in Mainline churches is classroom based and is designed to educate people *about* Christianity. It's the very Sunday school and Bible study mentality that has brought us to where we are today. We have some of the best educated church members on the planet – we certainly have access to a wealth of teaching resources. But this kind of discipleship will never win back the West. Disciple making may begin with training, but it can never end in a classroom. Sooner or later it must spill over into our everyday relationships where we share our faith. And we've been waiting for generations for that process to work … it's probably time to do something different.

Radical Discipleship is More than Learning Scripture

One example of misunderstanding the meaning discipleship has been perpetuated for decades by my tribe, United Methodists. We developed a program called *Disciple Bible*. The goal was to instill the basic kingdom concepts in the students, connect them with a spiritual director who helped connect their passion with a ministry, and then send them out to serve. However, *Disciple Bible I* was followed by *Disciple Bible II* and then *Disciple Bible III* and so on until a person can stay in the classroom for years and never become involved in a ministry where they could both live out their faith and learn the true meaning of discipleship. My denomination did this because it considered discipleship a form of education rather than a transformation of life and we have dearly paid the price.

Another example of misunderstanding the nature of discipleship is seen in the way Mainliners view small groups. Most Mainliners see small groups as Bible studies that educate people, when they are supposed to be transformative communities where people both learn and grow by doing. Transformational small groups emphasize learning from one another while applying the Scriptures to their everyday lives in their day-to-day words, actions, and attitudes. More on small groups later.

The Basic Tenets of Radical Discipleship

An understanding of Ephesians 4:11–12 is essential for any solid understanding of discipleship.[14] Among other things, (which are the fodder for another book[15]), this passage makes it clear that the role of the pastor is to equip the congregation and that the role of the congregation is to do the ministry. For some reason, Mainliners seem to have cut this text out of the Bible because it is so clear on the roles of pastor and congregation that it is impossible to see how we could have missed it. But when a congregation believes it's the role of the pastor to be the spiritual "hitman" instead of an equipper, radical discipleship is impossible.

So, here are the basic tenets of radical discipleship.

- Every person is considered to be a local missionary of the gospel instead of a member or worshipper;
- Everyone is responsible for one another instead of looking to the pastor to be a caregiver;
- Disciple making is a way of life that happens inside and outside of the church with attending a church service being a sidebar;
- No one is indispensable;
- Paid staff exist primarily to help people grow into what God intended them to be rather than being a chaplain or caregiver;
- Paid staff offer on-the-job training and mentoring and do little independent hands-on ministry;
- Every leader has an intern or two learning the trade of how to be a disciple of Jesus instead of merely sitting in a classroom soaking up the Bible;
- All leaders, and many in the congregation, live and breathe to encourage and equip every person to actively serve in God's mission by discipling and equipping others;

This view of the church is at the heart of a discipleship culture. But for such a culture to be developed and nurtured, paid staff and church leaders must have a different understanding of ministry and the roles played by paid staff and congregation. In short, paid staff must cease being doers of ministry

---

[14] And his gifts were that some should be apostles, some prophets, some evangelists, some pastors and teachers, to equip the saints for the work of ministry, for building up the body of Christ.

[15] See Alan Hirsch, *5Q Collective*.

and become equippers of ministry, and the congregation must stop relying on paid staff for everything and become the doers of ministry.

Two huge barriers stand in the way of to developing a discipleship culture:

- Pastors not willing to give up doing ministry; and
- Lay people not taking responsibility for the ministry.

These changes go against the norm in most Mainline churches. Too often pastors need to be needed so much that they can't give up ministry and many lay people think of their pastors as church employees or personal chaplains. These attitudes kill any hope of developing a culture of discipleship. They must cease. It's time for radical disciples to step forward.

Discipleship Pipeline – Not Drainpipe

If radical discipleship is the key to multiplication, then churches need to develop a discipleship pipeline. A discipleship pipeline is whatever method a church uses to move people from their seat to the street. This pipeline trains people to be disciple makers outside the four wall of the church. The heart and soul of every effective discipleship pipeline I've seen occurs on three fronts, which we'll examine in a minute:

- Minimal in-house formal training;
- One-on-one mentoring of an apprentice by someone further along in his or her faith;
- Active participation in a disciple-making small group.

It's rare for a person to become a radical disciple by spending one-hour-a-week attending a church service. Instead, radical discipleship requires face-to-face encounters that include spending time together, small groups, daily devotions, journaling, mentoring and ongoing assessment.

However, most Mainline ministries resemble a drainpipe rather than a pipeline. The laity runaround like chickens with their heads cut off going to one meeting after another, where little or nothing gets accomplished. All this kind of ministry does is drain the spiritual life out of a person. As a result, they:

- Seldom, if ever, invite their neighbors to join them in worship;
- Rarely, if ever, leave a meeting revved up to the point they can't wait to tell someone about their church;
- Usually look forward to the day they can hand over their position to some other unsuspecting newbie;
- Rarely reach any form of spiritual maturity where they are willing to sacrifice on behalf of others;
- Mostly give time and money out of duty;
- And rarely have time to be part of a transforming small group.

Notice the traditional members experience in most Mainline churches. The don't receive any mentoring and as soon as they show any signs of life they are put on a committee and if they faithfully attend meeting after meeting they may be made chairperson.

Contrast that with the discipleship pipeline that takes a person from being unchurched and carries them along until they become a sold-out disciple maker.

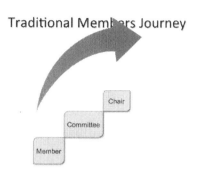

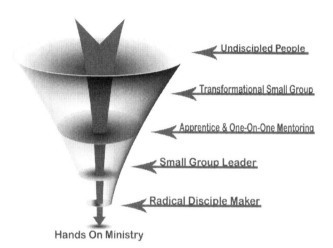

As a result, people are:

- So excited that they can't help but tell others about the joy and fulfillment they experience in their worship;
- Reluctant to give up whatever ministry they are involved in because it brings them such satisfaction;
- So mature that they are often willing to be sent out into the community to serve others;
- Great financial givers because they give out of appreciation for what God has done in their life and in the hope of furthering the kingdom;
- Able to mentor an unchurched person to the point of baptism;
- Responsible for their brothers and sisters rather than expecting the pastor to do it for them.

Three Components of Radical Discipleship

Although they vary in application of the components, every effective discipleship method we've seen consists of three parts: training, one-on-one mentoring, and transformational small groups.

Training

Training is the least important part of radical discipleship, but still necessary, especially with new people. Usually this training is either introducing new people to the church or teaching maturing Christians how to lead a small group. It is the least important component because discipleship isn't about how much we know but what we do with what we know.

I'm not downplaying education. Mainliners just do education all wrong. Of course, we need to know what Jesus taught, but more importantly we must be able to apply it to our everyday lives. Most Mainliners today have a head full of information about the Bible but little application beyond their own morality. But knowledge without application results in less than radical disciples. It's not what we know that will change the world; it's how we love others and share the Good News that will have ultimately win back the West for Christianity. If we focused on Jesus' new commandment: "Love one another as I have loved you," we wouldn't need much more education.

One-On-One Mentoring

Do you remember the old saying: "I do and you watch; You do and I watch; You do and someone else watches." Mentoring consists of mature disciples doing, and newer Christians watching and then debriefing. It's just like an apprentice learning a trade by watching a master craftsman. Mature leaders walk alongside their apprentices doing ministry together. It is one thing to hear about faith in the Scriptures, it's another to see it in action and become part of it. This form of learning is far superior to any classroom setting.

Don't be fooled – mentoring takes time. And in the beginning less ministry might get done. But mentors are willing to spend this time because they believe that the best form of leadership is that which results in the most ministry getting done through others rather than by them doing it. They know the more people they mentor the more ministry will be accomplished over the long haul. Thus, over time, multiplication will replace addition or decline.

Transformational Small Groups

It's been my experience that no matter how much training or one-on-one mentoring takes place, sooner or later most people become part of a transformational small group where people do life together and feel comfortable exploring their personal and spiritual issues as well as what it means to be a follower of Jesus. These groups usually have three goals: (1) to help people grow closer to Christ and to one another; (2) to provide a small community where everyone is known by name and feels safe; and (3) to mentor and raise up future leaders. Of course, there is Bible study, but the emphasis isn't what happens in the head but what happens in the heart.[16]

Application of the Bible is more important to these groups than mere knowledge of the Bible.[17] Learning how to be obedient to Jesus' commands is what these small groups are about. That's why they are called transformational small groups to differentiate them from the small groups we find in so many churches.

Perhaps the best way to describe radical discipleship is by sharing some questions that might be asked in these transformational small groups.[18]

- Where have I sinned today and what am I going to do about it?
- Am I willing to follow every command of my Lord and Savior?
- Am I willing to go wherever God asks me to go?
- What does it mean for me to give my life according to the demands of the gospel?
- How can my life be molded into the pattern of Jesus' servanthood?
- What are the daily implications of my loving my enemy?
- What temptations have I had today and what did I do about them?
- What is God doing in your life this week?
- Where are you struggling?
- How can we pray for you?

As you read these questions you can easily see why the normal Sunday school or Bible study is drastically different from transformational small groups.

By now you are aware that radical discipleship goes beyond what we see in most Mainline congregations. Radical discipleship is the process of being remade in the image of Christ. As Paul says, "Therefore, if anyone is in Christ, he is a **new** creation; the old has passed away, behold, the **new** has come." [19] Radical discipleship is being on the road to mission with Jesus. Radical discipleship is more than learning Scripture. It is being fashioned in the image

---

[16] For in depth help with small groups, you can purchase Missional Small Groups in our store at https://effectivechurch.net/store/missional-small-groups/

[17] These small groups are so important that some thriving churches make attending one a prerequisite to joining.

[18] I have adapted these questions from the works of both Wesley and the Anabaptists and added some myself.

[19] 2 Corinthians 5:17

of Jesus. No wonder the first Christians were called "followers of the Way."[20]

Sacred Cows Mainliners Must Get Over

The more I study Scripture through the lens of multiplication the more I realize that several sacred cows will have to be barbequed for multiplication to become a reality. These sacred cows are tough and will be hard to swallow. Let me share a few of the biggest ones I've repeatedly experienced through the years. Let me remind you to please keep two things in mind as you read this section: one, I've been a Mainline pastor for more than fifty years; and two, I only have one prayer for Mainline Christianity – that it will regain its former glory.

Seminary Training

A different understanding of pastoral education is needed for Mainline churches. Most Mainline denominations require seminary training, but Multiplication is much more difficult if pastors must go to seminary before leading a church. It takes too much time and too much money. But we don't have the time or money for that. We must find ways around this requirement.

A lesson from the past can show us the way. Prior to requiring seminary training, the Methodist Church was growing. But in the mid 1950s Methodist pastors were required to complete a seminary education and by the mid 1960s Methodism was in decline. Coincidence? I don't think so.

Give that some thought.

Of course, I can hear denominational officials screaming while reading this. But let me ask you, "How are things working out for you? Are your churches growing?"

I know this is hard for established denominational people to hear and I respect that. But I also have heartburn over the growing number of people in the West who aren't followers of Jesus. We can't let this escalation of non-Christians continue. We must do something; and that something is multiplication.

Ordination is Just for Trained Clergy

Ever hear someone say, "I'm just a layperson"? Usually that's an excuse to not take responsibility for some form of ministry. Every time I hear those words my blood boils. No one is *just* a layperson.

When ordination is reserved for clergy we make second class citizens out of the rest of the congregation and set pastors apart from the rest of the church. If we are going to use the word "ordination," it must apply to everyone. You were ordained at your baptism … and if you take Jeremiah

---

[20] Acts 19:2, 9, 23

and the psalmists seriously, you were ordained even before your birth! But Mainliners are hung up here. Why, I don't know. Ordination, as we use it today, isn't biblical.

We need a different understanding of ordination if multiplication is to happen. The church I attend when I'm in town has several pastors and only one of them is seminary trained, the others were ordained by that church based on their gifts, not their education. And this church is thriving.

Now I know for many leaders this sounds like heresy. But United Methodists especially should know the wisdom of what I'm saying about trained pastors. Methodists took the gospel from the east coast to the west coast through the work of uneducated Circuit Riders. Not much different from what I'm proposing. Drop seminary training and ordination based on education and start relying on ordination based on passion for people who don't yet know Jesus, a willingness to serve, and demonstrated results. Much of the rest of the world is already doing this and is thriving.

Making a distinction between clergy and laity is a killer for radical discipleship because it divides God's people into experts and novices. The use of the terms implies that clergy are the ones to do important ministries and the laity aren't expected to be radical disciples. But as long as clergy are looked up to as special people with special gifts multiplication will never happen. It's time we never hear again, "I'm just a lay person."

Treating Ministry as a Career

In many Mainline denominations, the goal of too many clergy is to keep their nose clean and move up the corporate ladder, getting a bigger church and salary. This minimizes the need for the pastor to do any effective ministry, much less multiply ministry. The new path for the future, however, is not career, but calling. Multiplication is the last place for pastors who want an easy path to job security.

Passion for Centralization and Control

We would do well to learn from the spontaneous expansion of the Church in China under Mao Zedong. The faith spread solely by word of mouth. Unfortunately, we'll never see a multiplication movement within Mainline denominations if we continue to view centralized structure and order as essential components of a church. Decentralization is important for a multiplication movement to occur. Radical disciples don't need checks and balances.

New Christians Must be Trained Before Sharing Their Faith

Every successful multiplication movement has recognized the power of a new Christian's passion to pass on what he or she has experienced. New converts must be encouraged from day one to share their faith with others because in doing so two things happen: One, the Good News is spread; and two, the new converts learn more about their faith. Indeed, new Christians must be encouraged from day one to share their faith while it's still red hot.

Protect Doctrine at All Costs

The gospel doesn't need protecting; it needs to be allowed to spontaneously spread. A lot of leaders feel that we shouldn't permit untrained new Christians to spontaneously share in teaching others what they have experienced until they have been trained. This is just another desire to exercise control over people.

In the early years of my ministry I had a couple of Lay Witness Missions in the church where I served Christ. Lay people from all over the country converged on our church for a weekend of teaching and preaching. Their theology was awful, but their passion for Jesus was off the chart. I remember one night my wife saying to me, "Are you going to continue allowing this terrible theology to be preached from your pulpit?" I replied, "Honey, I can correct the theology, but I can't teach such passion." One of the results of those two Lay Witness Missions was the church tripled in size in the following year.

"Volunteers" are Our Backbone

"Volunteer" is a four-letter word that needs to be ostracized for our vocabulary. For most volunteers, everything depends on the situation. They give you what they want to give you, when they want to give it to you, and how they want to give it to you. There is nothing radical about a volunteer. We don't need volunteers; we need servants, who are willing to follow the Master wherever he takes them, if we want to spawn a multiplication movement. I've often said "Ministry is too important to be left in the hands of mere volunteers."

We Can't Do Ministry Without Programs and Committees

How in God's name we devised such things as programs and committees I'll never know. I guess the Devil made us do it ☺. The problem with committees is that over time they take on a life of their own.

At the end of one of my consultations where I urged them to reduce their number of committees, an older lady who had been in the church for decades approached me with this question – "If we eliminate all the committees as you suggest, how will we know who is faithful or not?"

Let that sink in.

Her understanding of faithfulness was attending a committee, and she had been in the church for decades. That kind of understanding of discipleship won't get us very far. But it's helped get us where we are today.

Radical Discipleship and Multiplication

Why is radical discipleship so crucial to multiplication? Only radical disciples will respond to the call of church and God to go and do whatever is needed. Only radical disciples will stand up to the bullies and tell them where they can go – that is out of the church.[21] Only radical disciples will find ways to share their faith with their networks. And only radical pastors will be willing to measure their successes through the achievements of others. Now do you see why radical discipleship is the foundation and heart of any multiplication movement?

Final Thoughts on Radical Discipleship

My experience with young adults has taught me that they either commit to something 150 percent or they have nothing to do with it. There's not much middle ground to them. They already live in a world filled with too much gray. The last thing they want from Christianity is a middle of the road faith. They are looking for a solid, loving, and authentic community that will produce results. Either we produce churches with radical disciples or we will miss an entire generation of people and fail to win back the West.

---

[21] For more on how to deal with bullies, see Appendix A.

5
THE PRINCIPLES OF MULTIPLICATION

So, if you're still with us, and producing radical disciples is the heart of multiplication, what are some of the principles that make this kind of discipleship possible?

Multiplication can occur if the following principles are consistently honored.

A commitment to Jesus Christ as Lord and Savior of the world is the spark that lights the fire of this movement.

We begin with this principle because of the large number of Mainline Christians who question the deity and lordship of Jesus Christ. For this movement to take hold, Jesus is either Lord and Savior of the world or the movement will die for lack of the kind of passion that can keep it going. Radical disciples understand that Jesus is the sole authority for everything in their daily life from sex to money, from diet to career. This is the starting point of all true disciple making and eliminates the consumer mentality that plagues Mainline churches. Multiplication begins and ends here.

Kingdom is more important than church.

Mainline pastors must get over their passion for "church," "turf," and "membership." A simple story will illustrate what I mean.

I was working in an Eastern seaboard state helping some United Methodists plot out locations to plant churches. Their Conference had been on the decline for decades and had recently began a freefall decline. I had spent several days looking at the demographics as well as the locations of their existing churches. We found several dozen locations that desperately needed a new church. Our two criteria were: one, the area was growing; and two, there wasn't a growing United Methodist Church in the area. On the surface, what we proposed was a no-brainer.

However, each proposed location was met with serious pushback. "We can't put a church there. It's too close to one of our existing churches." Now remember, all the existing churches were dying. Most had only a couple of dozen people in attendance and were being subsidized by the Conference. We pushed back and asked them to invite the effected pastors to a meeting to discuss the possibility of planting these new churches in their area. We hoped we would find some kingdom minded pastors in the group. But you guessed it. Every pastor was outraged at the thought of planting a new church in their area, even though their churches were dying. As a result, the Conference rejected our plan and continued its death spiral. These pastors and this Conference put "church" before the "kingdom." I have repeatedly run into this response over the years.

Putting more emphasis on church encourages a hunker-in-the-bunker mentality and keeps members bottled up within the four walls instead of sending them out into the community. Putting church over kingdom results in an emphasis on members rather than disciples, programs rather than ministries, control rather than freedom, turf rather than world, programs for members instead of ministries that reach out to the lost, and worst of all-engrains a survival mentality.

Reliance on individuals to share their faith with their everyday networks.

The rapid expansion of the church in the early centuries was due to the activities of individuals sharing the faith as they went about their daily lives. People saw in them something they did not have and they wanted it. Every time they shared their faith they learned something new about their faith and themselves and they grew in faith. The more they shared it, the better they became at sharing it. The better they became, the easier it was to share. Over time, sharing their faith became a normal part of their life, even in the face of danger. The same must happen today. Since new converts are normally the most passionate individuals in the church, they should be encouraged to share their faith the very first day of their new life. Like the woman at the well who ran to tell everyone what Jesus had said to her, new converts should be encouraged to share their faith.

An unapologetic reliance on non-seminary trained pastors.

Any form of effective multiplication will outgrow the number of formally trained and ordained clergy. But that's okay because early Christianity grew on the backs of everyday people, and if we are going to fuel this movement we will have to do the same. This means that everyone in a congregation must be considered a potential missionary to their community. The congregation must see themselves as a "Go" congregation where everyone is expected to invest themselves fully in the lives of others.

Because of the reliance of this movement on the Holy Spirit, and not a denomination or program, there is no way for anyone to control how and where it expands.

Control, by its very nature, rules out multiplication. The actions of God are always out of our control. Those who understand this are admittedly plagued by fear. No one wants to lose control, especially denominational leaders. But giving up control is precisely what we must do. We must trust the Spirit to do its work while we do ours. Unfortunately, it's this inability to control the movement that is one of the reasons why accepting multiplication is so difficult for Mainline leaders.

For multiplication to happen, churches must be self-supporting, self-governing, and self-expanding. Heavy, top down control is deadly. Any attempt by a denomination to intervene in any way puts the brakes on multiplication. Of course, encouragement is critical; but intrusion isn't. Yes, there will be mistakes along the way. Churches and individuals will fail. But we dare not allow our fear of failure to dampen the movement. We should be more afraid of squelching the movement than we are of having to endure a few failures along the way.

A core belief that every person in the church is expected to become a neighborhood missionary.

Every member understands that he or she is expected to be an active kingdom builder; that there is no distinction between clergy and laity and God is calling them to be more than a church member. These churches not only expect this, they actively and intentionally train their people to take such leadership. We must reach the place where those who are *not* sharing their faith become uncomfortable because, in their perception, *everyone* else in the church is sharing.

We are past the time when we need to think like pastors. The context today demands that we function and think like missionaries in a foreign land. Our focus must not be our church, but what happens when our people journey out beyond the four walls of our churches. They must be trained to take the gospel to the people. It's not a matter of "if we are called;" it's "to what have we been called?" If there is to be a multiplication movement, it will be done through everyday Christians. The new metric for success is how many disciples make other disciples.

Adaptive and empowering systems that have a bias toward freedom and innovation.

In a world like the one we are called upon to minister in today any effective multiplication movement must champion innovation, freedom, and risk. A multiplication movement today will require a spontaneous, uncontrolled ability to multiply. Remember, we must think like rabbits, not dinosaurs. These systems must be able to quickly adapt to the constant changes of our world. Disciples must be free to experiment with new forms of church that may not have any similarity to the past.[22]

Reflections

Leaders who want multiplication aren't about growing their church as much as they are about change – change in people and in society. The Great Commission overshadows all they do. Everything is predicated on a "Go" mentality. They barely count the number of people in worship; they count the number of people they have sent into the community.

Now you have some insight into what it takes to experience multiplication. My tribe, The United Methodist Church, was built on many of these principles. When Asbury and Coke stood on the eastern shore of North America, the only theology that meant anything to them was "How do we get the gospel from the East Coast to the West Coast?" From that vision, the Circuit Rider was born. Circuit Riders didn't have a head office with whom they could communicate. There was no central command center. They weren't theological scholars. All they had was a horse, a Bible, and a whole lot of faith. And through the Circuit Rider, Methodism planted the first church in almost every village and town from the East Coast to the West Coast. It's time for another such movement to catch fire.

---

[22] For more on this culture, see Bill Easum, *Sacred Cows Make Gourmet Burgers*. You can purchase an electronic version in our store or a print copy through Amazon.

6
CREATING A MULTIPLICATION CULTURE

"If you want to change the culture,
you will have to start by changing the organization."
Mary Douglas

Disciple making can't be just another fad of the moment. It must become the culture of a multiplying church.

Culture is the intersection at what a church does and who a church is. Culture is how a people live and what they do. Culture determines everything an organization achieves. It's more important than strategy; in fact, it eats strategy faster than a kid eats ice cream. Culture is the unseen force that fans the flames of commitment. It is what allows churches to move from addition to multiplication.

Culture isn't something you can explain but you know it when you experience it. It's not something you can put on paper and carry around with you. People simply must experience it to know it. And that's what makes culture impossible to fake.

Perhaps the culture of Mainline Denominations can best be described as museumesque. Our churches maintain carefully curated traditions, rites, and rituals. From the music we sing and the instruments that accompany them, to the creeds and prayers and litanies we recite, virtually everything we do is anachronistic. Instead of excited, joy-filled conferences, our "worship services" are staid, tired, and anchored heavily in decades or centuries gone by. The most life an average congregation sees is when some upstart pastor tries to change or rearrange something in the museum. At that moment, the patrons who have bought and paid for the church's stability rise up to restore good order, maintain decorum, and reestablish tradition. The members largely see themselves as docents and hosts whose job is to interpret the experience and, at the end of the day, they return to their homes content that they have done all that's been asked of them … they have maintained the church's culture for another week. Any outsiders who make their way into these churches may leave with a sense of awe and appreciation for the arts, but are otherwise untouched, uninspired, and unchanged because the experience was designed to educate, not transform.

Corporate culture is the intersection of vision, values, narrative, leaders, and practices that characterize and guide an organization. Let's look at each one.[23]

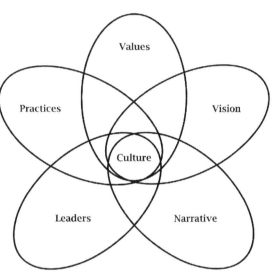

Values

Values are the bedrock of everything – what we talk about, what we do, who we select and disciple as leaders, and how we spend our money. A church's values are the core of its culture. Jim Collins calls values the "guiding principles" of an organization.[24] Whereas, a vision articulates a church's destination, values offer a set of guidelines on the behaviors and mindsets needed to achieve that vision. You can tell what a person's or church values are by watching what they do and how they invest their resources. Their actions betray their values.

Today, the values of most Mainline Denominations at best, center around social programs, and at worst center around survival, neither of which provides the spark for multiplication.

A few years ago, I was consulting with a church that said it wanted to grow. They said they were a church whose passion was to develop fully devoted disciples of Jesus. On Sunday morning as I was evaluating their worship service I was shocked to hear them begging for people to sign up to teach Sunday School. You don't have to beg fully devoted disciples to do anything. I later learned the pastor borrowed this phrase from Willow Creek. It wasn't a value embedded deep in his soul; it didn't reflect the values of the

---

[23] I'm indebted to Todd Wilson for some of the use of values, narrative, and behavior.
[24] Jim Collins and Jerry I. Porras, "Building Your Company's Vision," *Harvard Business Review*, Reprint #96501.

staff or the congregation and therefore it was worthless. It had no bearings on the actions and vision of the church.

Our values will always generate personal and corporate action. If this pastor really lived and breathed developing fully devoted disciples they wouldn't have to beg from the pulpit. They would disciple people in the trenches until they were fully devoted disciples who would move heaven and earth to disciple others.

Vision

A great culture depends on a clear, compelling, and inspiring vision. Vision is guided by the church's values and provides the church with direction and purpose. When it's authentic and embedded in the leaders, it acts as a compass for the church. Most Mainline Denominations no longer live by their original vision of making disciples that change the world, a vision that once made them a relevant force in society. Now that the original vision is lost, they are all in decline and need to recover their original vision. Think back … what was the original vision of your tribe and how do you recover it?

Practices

Values are of little importance unless they result in action. Remember the phrase, "They will know we are Christians by our love"? Churches that are less than loving, who harbor bullies and terrorists, and tolerate bad behavior betray their values by their actions – or inactions, as the case may be.

Multiplying churches don't multiply because they have created great values and a great vision. They're multiplying churches because they've put into practice what they say they value in order to reach the vision they say they yearn for. The pastor spends more time with the unchurched than with the saints. The church board spends more time doing mission than evaluating and planning and organizing and talking about it. And church members are in the church building just long enough to be re-inspired and re-equipped to share yet another breakthrough faith story with their unchurched and irreligious friends. Without faithful practices, there is no multiplication.

Narrative

We talk about what we value. We tell stories about what we value. And we make heroes out of those who do what we value. Pastors who value multiplication talk about it with the same fervor that they talk about their favorite sports team. They share stories of multiplication, they celebrate, and they make heroes out of those individuals involved in multiplication.

And where do they get these stories? From their own practices, from the practices of the church's leaders, and from the practices of the typical church member. When a congregation values discipleship and life-transformation, it puts their values and vision into practice. And when they engage in faith-filled practices, they get results. And from those results, they get stories … stories that become the narrative building blocks for multiplication.

If you listen carefully to the conversations within the ranks of many Mainline pastors you will hear a narrative that focuses on pension, budgets, membership, survival, and the desire for a bigger church. This type of narrative doesn't instill a passion to reach the lost.

Never underestimate the power of telling the stories that lead up to the decision to become a multiplying church. They are some of the most moving and compelling tools you have.

So, begin to archive stories that illustrate multiplication. Stories that share why you do what you do, who you it for, why you're passionate about it, and where the church is headed. Many of these stories will naturally come out of your small groups, so encourage the small group leaders to share them with you regularly.

Leaders

Culture comes from the top and runs down throughout the church. It is highly unlikely that healthy culture is the result of consensus or team effort, and good culture never reaches up from the bottom. That's why the actions of the Lead Pastor are such a determining factor in church multiplication. If this person doesn't eat, sleep, and breathe multiplication it won't happen. The more consistent the Lead Pastor's actions are, the more likely multiplication is to occur.

Mainline structures often hamper pastors from being a strong enough leader to be able to set culture. The checks and balances on a pastor's leadership are enormous. It's as if the congregation is so afraid the pastor will do something bad that they ensure he or she can do nothing good. And in the absence of a strong leader, negative people step into the vacuum and stifle the church's progress.

But it takes more than just a committed pastor to set a culture. That's why it's so important to ensure every staff member, every appointed leader, and even every nominated leader embraces the church's vision, embodies the values, and implements the expected behaviors and covenants. If the leadership team doesn't epitomize the desired culture, a consumer "what about me?" culture will fill the void.

No church can build a coherent culture without leaders and followers who share the core values. That's why most effective multiplication churches raise up their leaders from within their small groups. Bringing on the right "culture carriers" reinforces the existing culture and gives the church a chance to multiply.

Your Church's Culture Can Be Changed

Culture isn't quick setting concrete. It's more like lead – give it enough heat and you can mold it into something new. You can change or recreate your church's culture. That's what happens when a dying church is revitalized. The culture is changed. So, there's hope for every church. All you have to do is turn up the heat!

How can culture be changed?

- Start living out in practice what it means to be an equipper rather than a doer and don't be intimidated when members complain. Remember, you are the curriculum. What they see you do is more important than what they learn in a course – or even hear in a sermon.
- Quit trying to get people involved in committees, programs, and even worship. Instead, equip your people to serve others and send them out into the community.
- Limit the number of committees and focus most of your ministries on the community.
- Quit trying to educate people into the kingdom, instead connect them with effective mentors who will work with them in the trenches.
- Start loving one another and your neighbor more than you love yourself.
- Make sure bullies know that their behavior won't be tolerated and if their behaviors persist, show them the door.
- Make small groups that produce reproducing disciples the heart of your ministry so that you are a church *of* small groups rather than a church *with* small groups.
- Measure the number of new disciples and apprentices that are emerging each month and make that measure more important than counting the offering.
- See everyone in your church as a potential neighborhood missionary.
- Make sure your staff is equippers not doers and quickly replace those who can't make the shift.
- Don't blink when opposition arises (notice I said "when" not "if.")
- And pray like mad.

7

TRANSITIONING TO MULTIPLICATION

If you are still with me, the multiplication bug has probably bitten you, and you're interested in learning how to move in that direction. Excellent!

Remember, multiplication won't happen overnight nor will it be an easy journey. You probably have a few sacred cows you need to barbeque first and a lot of naysayers to overcome. Moving from wherever you are to multiplication means you're going to have to make some radical changes that will affect everything you are and ever will be. If you're up for that, read on. The journey will be worth it.

At the heart of multiplication is a fundamental shift from the Addition Culture of gathering and accumulating people to a Multiplication Culture of mentoring, discipling, and sending. And if you're ready and willing to take a stab at creating such a culture here's where you begin.

The Starting Line

Dream for a moment that you are standing by a pond and you have a rock in your hand. You throw it into the lake and it causes ripples that expand outward like an ever-widening circle. In a slow methodical fashion, the ripples will expand to fill the pond. It will take some time, but the ripples always extend beyond the initial ripple.

Now picture the rock as the representative of your vision to shift from addition to multiplication. The ripples represent the changes you must go through to bring your vision to reality. The transition will be a long, slow process. To achieve the vision of multiplication you'll have to hang onto the dream like a junkyard dog with a T-bone steak it stole off the grill.

The biggest obstacle you'll face will probably be the tradition and practices (culture) of your church and denomination. Long-time members and denominational leaders have an extensive history of not wanting to change anything, much less rock the boat. They have done things the way they are doing them for so long they can't imagine doing anything differently. They

are living in a history museum that is committed to protecting its history and its traditions. But it's your job to step outside the box and take the risk of doing things that will lead to multiplication. So, here's some of the crucial things you need to do:

Ripple 1: Admit that Multiplication is Over Your Head

Let's be honest. Transitioning a Mainline church into one that grows by multiplication is a monumental task that only God can accomplish. It's a God thing. It's not about you.

So, that's where we must begin, with acknowledging our total dependence on God. If we fail to do this, we will fall on our face. I've always said, "If it's possible, God probably isn't in it. But if it is impossible, you can be sure God is near, ready to hold your hand because you never know what's possible until you take a step beyond what is possible."

Help your people know that fear of change is normal. Share with them that you too are experiencing some of the same angst they are feeling. Covenant with them to pray for strength and guidance as you move forward.

And for God's sake, don't take anything personal along the way. You've got to be better than that. But be just as aware that there are those in your congregation who will do their best to try and make it be "all about you." Keep pointing to Jesus, keep reaching the unreached, and get a coach who will keep you focused on what's really important … changing the church's culture to following the Way of discipleship and multiplication.

Ripple 2: Change the Way You Process Mission

The focus of most effective Mainline pastors is accumulation – getting butts in the seats. It's ingrained in our thinking. But we must challenge that kind of thinking and replace it with a multiplication mindset. The focus of all future training must be discipleship, not accumulation. We must begin to value raising up leaders who will disciple rather than increasing our worship attendance. We must think "going" instead of "attracting." And here's the kicker – doing so will result in more people coming to Christ which results in more people in worship.

In your next staff meeting talk about disciple making. Every week ask how many new disciples have been raised up. Forget about the budget or worship and evaluate everything through the lens of discipleship and multiplication.

Ripple 3: Make Disciple Making Your #1 Focus and Limit Your Number of Ministries

Do not base your ministry on "find a need and fill it" because if you do you will have too many ministries that will divert your focus from discipling. Discontinue those ministries that do not produce new leaders/disciples. That means you will need to eliminate most, if not all, of the regular programs and committees and replace them with ministries that disciple people.

Eliminating most ministries sounds counterproductive. That's because we've based ministry on getting people active. We've believed if we keep them involved, they will show up in worship. But history has shown involvement doesn't result in devoted disciples. It may keep them busy for a while but it doesn't disciple them.

Ripple 4: Change the Way You Behave

Moving from addition to multiplication begins in a change of mind and ends in execution of that change. This transition is behavior modification. It's about how we act and what we do, not what we think. We can't *think* ourselves into a new culture. We must practice it. We must live out a multiplication culture. That means how we allocate our time, money and energy must be channeled into actions that lead to multiplication. We must become uncomfortably discontent with mere addition no matter how successful our addition growth might be.

Multiplication depends on what is in our heart and how that directly affects our behavior. There is no church growth formula we can follow. At the heart of this movement is a red-hot passion to see the Great Commission fulfilled in our lifetime and it will be this passion that drives who we are, what we do, and what we dream about.

Ripple 5: Change the Way You Measure Success

If you don't measure something, you don't value it, so what you measure is important. The success of multiplication can't be measured by our worship attendance or the size of your budget. Doing so keeps us victims to an addition culture, and as important as attendance and budgets are, they're not the heart of the gospel. Success needs to be measured by how many people are discipled and sent into ministry.

Scorecards are valuable in any game because they tell you if you're winning. If it is important to know if you're winning in a game, how much more important is it to know if you are winning as a church. So let me suggest a new score card keeping in mind you should measure attendance and income, but these should be secondary measurements.

So, what would our new scorecard include?

- How many new Christians do we have this year? In other words, the number of adult conversion baptisms that we've done. The ultimate practice of the Great Commission is to engage in the politically incorrect practice of conversions, evangelism, and sharing the salvation that comes from believing and following Jesus. And the ultimate fruit is newly baptized believers.[25]

- How many disciples do we have this year? We define a disciple as someone being apprenticed to become more like Jesus in *every* aspect of their lives. Apprenticing is learning the "Jesus trade."

- How many of our people are being mentored? Do each of our leaders have several apprentices learning the Jesus trade? And are the apprentices learning how to be a neighborhood missionary?

- How many of our people are we sending out to connect with lost people? It doesn't matter what you are sending them out to do if it results in four things: (1) it blesses those being served; (2) it blesses those serving; (3) it creates visibility for the church; and finally, (4) it results in growing the kingdom of God with new disciples.

---

[25] A note for our confessional church friends: Dependency on biological growth, that is, baptizing the little children of our church members, has failed the Western Church. Most children raised in a local church, leave the wider Church completely ... and research to date shows that they are not returning even after they've had children of their own. If we're going to turn the Western Church around, it will because we've shifted our focus and reallocated our resources to conversion evangelism. And that means counting conversion baptisms as our first measure of effectiveness.

Ripple 6: Develop a Discipleship Pipeline and Raise the Bar for Everyone

I touched on the Discipleship Pipeline back in Chapter 4. Few churches develop a clear, step-by-step discipleship pathway. As a consequence, no one is quite sure what it takes to lead one of their never-churched friends into full faith. There's an old adage, "If you don't have a plan to succeed, then you plan to fail." What's your plan for discipleship success? If you haven't created your church's pipeline, then it's time.

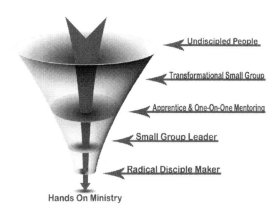

The illustration above is a simple pipeline that begins with undiscipled people and walks them through a disciple-making process. In reality, not every step will be made in order, but rarely do we find someone moving from far-from-God to Radical Disciple Maker without engaging in a life-transforming small group and experiencing one-on-one apprenticeship.

When introducing the pipeline, it's helpful if you can get your key leaders to engage the process *as if* they were brand new disciples. That's because, in my experience, that most Mainline church members – even if they're in leadership – are still baby disciples that are hooked on milk. By getting them to engage the process, you'll have an easier time of creating a disciple-making culture in your congregation.

When you do roll out your pipeline, be sure to raise the expectation level so that everyone who participates knows they will be sent out to disciple others in some capacity. Teach it at the new member's class. Preach it every Sunday. Make it part of your everyday conversations. In other words, live and breathe the Great Commission.

Ripple 7: Change How You Spend Your Time

Mainline pastors spend too much time focusing on the needs of the congregation when they should emphasize and prioritize a more outward focus. We should spend most of our time identifying and equipping people who are willing and able to mentor other new Christians or go into the community to serve. All our time should be spent getting our congregation to the point that it is reaching out.

This change in how we spend our time means your congregation will begin hearing stories about how the pastor and the church leaders are sharing their faith with those far from God. And when the church's leadership is prioritizing their time to share the Great Commission, it's more likely others will follow.

Ripple 8: Change the Way You Do Outreach/Evangelism

Inviting friends to worship is a good start, but it doesn't go far enough. Today we must encourage and train our people to share the gospel with their networks right where they are in their own world because the bulk of the population no longer attends church on their own. We must become backyard, neighborhood, and workplace missionaries. Programs like "Back to Church Sunday" just help fuel the addition culture. It's not very fearful to invite someone to church, but sharing faith with someone can cause the hair on the back of your neck to stand up on end. But doing so is the backbone of any multiplication movement – and there is no better feeling than when you help someone experience the life-transforming grace of Jesus Christ.

Ripple 9: The Way Staff Functions Must Change.

Instead of staff being focused mostly on caring for the flock, all staff must be focused on discipling the flock to be sent back into the community to share the gospel. They will need to be mentors more than administrators or program directors.

Ripple 10: The Way We Staff Must Change

For many Mainline churches this may be the proverbial rock wall. Most Mainline churches have some form of committee, council, or board that oversees the hiring and firing of paid staff. On the surface this may sound like a good idea, but it's not. All it does is water down the effectiveness of the staff and makes it harder to hold anyone accountable. Hiring and firing should be the prerogative of the Lead Pastor or Executive Pastor. The only person who should be accountable to a committee, council, or board is the Lead Pastor. All other staff ultimately should be the Lead Pastor's responsibility.

Why is this so important? Because multiplication depends on the staff being a team of people who respect each other, like one another, and have complimentary skill sets. They must be able to work in tandem with each other. And they must be able to respond quickly to major issues. When an outside group gets involved in personnel issues, teamwork and accountability are adversely affected. Transference often replaces accountability. "Trying really hard" replaces "results" as the measure of success. Besides, no one needs more than one supervisor, with the sole exception of the Lead Pastor.

So, if a church wants to move toward multiplication it must allow the Lead Pastor to lead the staff, which means no committees, teams, or boards intervening in the hiring, firing, or supervision of the staff members. The only time the church steps in is to hold accountable or to fire the Lead Pastor.

The Result of Making the Transition from Addition to Multiplication

The Church Becomes a Mentoring Center

Because of the emphasis on disciple making, the church becomes a mentoring center instead of a teaching or program based church. An emphasis on *learning about* the faith is replaced with an emphasis on *doing* faith. The only programs a church has are those that either train, mentor, or send people into the streets to share their faith.

Neighborhoods are the Prime Evangelism Thrust

The most effective evangelism is word of mouth. As consumers are transformed into disciples, they spread the gospel through their networks. The emphasis is no longer training laity to do the work of the church; now the emphasis is on equipping them to do the work of the kingdom in their neighborhood.

The Metric of Success is Effectiveness Outside the Campus

Because of the emphasis on sending, the primary metric for measuring success is a demonstrated impact on the community beyond the campus. Worship attendance is still important, but not as important as the impact the church makes outside its four walls.

Multiplication Becomes Decentralized and Spontaneous

Strategic plans take a back seat to uncontrollable, demonstrated, and spontaneous multiplication of all kinds and multiplication runs free without the constraints of top-down control, or even checks and balances.

The Priesthood of the Believer Replaces the Clergy/Laity Distinction

In the end, an emphasis on the priesthood of the everyday person will fuel the movement. Of course, we will still be plagued with ordained clergy, but now they aren't seen as the special ones who handle all the spiritual issues. Instead, the bulk of ministry is done by the laity who have been equipped to serve by being in the trenches alongside their mentor. The only time clergy are found doing hands-on ministry is in the early days when they are the only mentor.[26]

The Stress of Transitioning

Will transition from addition to multiplication be stressful? Yes, there will be many stressful moments. Is the pastor a shepherd or missionary? Is the focus on us or on them? Are we willing to risk making the internal changes necessary to move from addition to multiplication? Do the staff and I have the desire and ability to mentor? Will we shift the bulk of our budget, including missions, from maintenance to local outreach? The decisions will be endless in the early going of the transition. And the more effective a church has been in addition, the greater the tension will be. But over time the stress will turn into joy over the number of adult baptisms. If we want to win back the West, we must make the shift

Here's Your Transition Checklist

1. Make the initial commitment to multiplication, keeping in mind all the ripples listed above. Don't sugar coat the difficulties, but let everyone know you will walk alongside them.
2. Let your people know that your heart is broken over the lost condition of individuals and start demonstrating that concern.
3. Make discipleship the essential part of your DNA. Make it a central part of your membership training. And make it part of your monthly evaluation of your ministry. Talk about it all the time.
4. Stop thinking like a pastor and start thinking like a missionary. Pastors focus on their church; missionaries focus on the city.
5. Participate with another church that is already on its way to multiplication and learn from them.
6. Start looking for interns who are open to be radically discipled. These folks must be your best and brightest. They may even be some of your present staff members.
7. *Just do it!*

---

[26] If you're wondering what effective clergy do with all their time, if not doing hands on ministry, please see our book *Effective Staffing for Vital Churches* (Grand Rapids: Baker Publishing Group, 2012).

Time to Take the Leap

As you can see, making the shift from addition to multiplication is a really big risk. In fact, it is the biggest risk you will probably ever consider. Some might even call it "rolling the dice." After all, you must pay the bills to stay in ministry, don't you? What if it doesn't work? Just remember this is a faith issue. It's not supposed to be easy.

Taking a leap of faith is never easy, so I would encourage you to listen to Jesus once more – *"Go make disciples of all people groups."* Then choose the best way to do that and it will be clear – multiplication is the way to go.

Folks, it's time we all owned up to the fact that we are losing the battle for the West. The population is growing at a much faster rate than the number of new Christians. We can't go on doing what we've been doing and expect to survive much less thrive. We have only one chance – do what is necessary to make obedient Jesus followers who are willing to do whatever to win back the West. That is our only hope and it is a God-given hope we dare not ignore.

For those of you who are in thriving churches, I implore you to consider moving to multiplication. You may be doing well, but overall you are losing the battle. Let me ask you – how many people can you reach by doing what you're doing now compared to what you could accomplish if you raised up a large cadre of people who were willing to be sent to spread the word? What if a larger majority of your congregation felt the compulsion to go into the community and share their faith? Would that change the trajectory of your growth and the growth of the kingdom? If you believe so, then take the leap.

8
GOING FORWARD

Hopefully you've concluded that multiplication is a mindset and *the* way to do ministry and not merely a program or model. It's a new world view, a new way of living that's on fire to reach as many people as possible in the shortest amount of time. As such it can embrace several model strategies to consider:

1. **Multi-Site:** If you decide to use this model, see Appendix B
2. **Church Planting**: If you decide to use this model see *From Scarcity to Abundance: Creating a Culture of Multiplication*[27]
3. **Transformation Small Groups:** If you decide to use this model see Missional Small Groups[28]

I'm sure you can come up with many more ways to multiply the impact of your church or denomination. But the point is we don't have to settle for the status quo.

- It's time we quit thinking the new norm for our denominations is survival, plateau or decline.
- It's time we cared more about the lost than our members.
- It's time we came down off our clergy high horse and became one of the gang.
- It's time we ceased begging people to come to our worship services.
- It's time to replace the endless, mind-numbing committees with hands-on ministries that don't change people's lives.

---

[27] Available from Exponential at https://exponential.org/resource-ebooks/from-scarcity-to-abundance/
[28] Available at https://effectivechurch.net/store/missional-small-groups/

- It's time we valued transformation over education and freedom over control.
- It's time we learned that more leaders are grown in small groups than Sunday School.
- It's time to do everything in our power to help every individual in our congregations reach their full potential.
- It's time we put discipleship before everything else.

All of this can happen if we develop a multiplication mindset.

So what are you waiting for?

APPENDIX A

On Not Being Nice for the Sake of the Gospel

By Bill Easum

Throughout all my consulting ministry, I have seen a disturbing pattern ... most established churches are held hostage by one or two bullies. Some individual or small group of individuals are usually extremely opposed to the church making any radical change, even if it means the change would give the church a chance to thrive once again. I keep hearing pastors say, "*If I tried that, I'd lose my job!*"

Courageous pastors often ask, "What do I do when one person intimates the church so much that it is not willing to try something new?" My response is always, "Either convert them, neutralize them, or kick them out. The Body cannot live with cancer." To which someone usually cries, "That's not very Christian!"

My response describes much of the wisdom of both the Old Testament and Jesus. Maturing Christians love so deeply that they will do anything, even not being nice, "*for the sake of the Gospel.*" Jesus was so compassionate toward others that he could not remain quiet when he saw people holding other people in bondage.

The Old Testament story of the wilderness wanderings contains a remarkable account of how Moses responded to a group of people who insisted on keeping the Hebrews bondage to the past.[29] A group of people led by Korah came to Moses asking him to relinquish leadership because they wanted to take the Hebrews back to Egypt. Moses responded by falling on his face prostrate before them in prayer. Then he got up and slew all of them. Not very nice, but necessary if they were going to get to Canaan. Moses knew

---

[29] Numbers 16

that freedom with God was better than slavery with Pharaoh. The same is true today ... freedom to grow in grace is always better than enslavement to the status quo.

Almost every struggling church has at least one dysfunctional bully who goes out of the way to be a big fish in a small pond. Often, that is the primary reason the church is struggling. This person gets his/her sense of self-worth by keeping the church so intimidated, either by their actions or their money, that very little can happen without that person's approval. The sad thing is most of the leaders know that this person is a stumbling block to the church's future and they will not do anything about it. The church leaders ignore the bully thinking that is the Christian thing to do, and in so doing, assist in the stunted growth or death of the congregation.

For example, I was working with a staff in a large church. The first day I met with the staff the tension was so high I could cut the air with a knife. The staff hardly said a word to one another. The next day when we met the staff laughed and cut up together as if they were one big happy family. As I looked around the table, the only apparent difference was that one staff person was not present. I asked the staff if they sensed the difference I was feeling. They knew exactly what I meant. Finally one of them blurted out, "*Jim is not here today. Staff meetings are always better when he's not here.*" It turned out that Jim was a dysfunctional bully who ran to the personnel committee every time he didn't get his way. Because of him, several competent staff members had been fired. To make matters worse, the staff knew that Jim seldom contributed anything to the health and vitality of the church.

I asked the staff if they had confronted Jim with how they felt. Their response was typical for church folks. "*That would not be the Christian thing to do. It would hurt him deeply. After all, the church is all he has.*" Sure, it's all that he has; no one else would put up with him. Who is the most dysfunctional, Jim or the staff?

A church not far from me told its Bishop that it wanted a young pastor. It wasn't long before they got one. One of the first things the young pastor did was ask the Board to change the appearance of the church newspaper. The Board unanimously voted to do so. Four months later, I noticed the newspaper was switched back to its old form. I called the pastor to ask why. His response is a classic. "Most of the Board were present the night we voted. However, one man was out of the country. When he returned to find that a decision had been made in his absence, he demanded that the chairperson immediately call another meeting. At the second meeting, the Board voted unanimously to rescind their previous decision about the newspaper." When I asked why, he replied: "This man always pays off any deficit at the end of year and he wanted the vote changed. The Board was afraid to buck him." The future of that church was held hostage to a bully.

I'm convinced that one of the main sins of the established church is that we have taught ourselves to be nice instead of being Christian. In spite of aspiring to be a disciple of Jesus, we teach that the essence of Christianity is to be nice. Where do we get such a notion? Certainly not from the actions of Jesus.

One of the hallmarks of Jesus' ministry was his constant attack on the status quo. He challenged it every time he could. He even went out of his way to upset the religious bullies of his time. He called them whitewashed sepulchers and by doing so attacked the very heart of their priesthood based on purity.[30] Jesus loved church leaders too much to allow them remain such small persons. When Peter showed his displeasure over the impending death of his Lord, Jesus said to him "*Get behind me Satan.*"[31] Jesus loved his disciples too much to let them miss one of the more important lessons of servanthood. Jesus, the man who said, "*be compassionate as God is compassionate,*"[32] had no desire to be nice because ... being nice has nothing to do with being Christian. Being nice is often nothing more than a lack of compassion for people. Let's explore what this means.

At one point, in a holy rage, Jesus entered the Temple with a large, metal-tipped whip and drove out the money changers. As he did, he quipped, "*It is written, My house shall be called the house of prayer; but you have made it a den of thieves.*"[33] If we discover why Jesus responded to religious bullies this way, we will also discover why so many church leaders refuse to follow his example.

When Jesus cleansed the temple he was in the Court of the Gentiles. This was the only part of the temple where Gentiles were allowed to worship. What ticked Jesus off was that the religious leaders were monopolizing the only place Gentiles could worship God as the place to sell their wares. What was to be a place of spiritual discovery and worship for the Gentiles, was turned into an economic opportunity for the religious leaders (sound familiar?). The focus of the religious leaders was on themselves, not the spiritual vitality of the Gentiles. So he drove them out.

Therefore, by definition here, thieves are those who do religious things for their own purpose. So when we are doing things that only benefit those within the church, we become a den of thieves. When we say that we want it this way because it has always been this way, we are a den of thieves. When focus only on the needs of our members, we are robbing the community of a chance to join us in the journey of faith. Such action is intolerable for people of compassion and love.

[30] Matthew 23:27
[31] Matthew 16:23
[32] Luke 6:36
[33] Matthew 21:13

Church leaders are robbing people of their spiritual birthright when they allow dysfunctional people to sell their petty wares in the house of God rather than to proclaim release from bondage. We really need to get clear on this problem and do something about it. If we really love people, and if we really want them to experience the love of God, then we will not ever allow a bully to rob others of their spiritual birthright. Anyone who knows how family systems work, knows that the worst thing one can do with dysfunctional people is to give them attention by giving into their every whim. Instead, tough love has to be applied. The compassionate thing to do is to hold them accountable for their self-centered actions, for in doing so they may begin the journey with God.

Jesus shows us what to do with people who do not want to grow spiritually. In training his disciples how to spread the word of God's love, he told the disciples to "shake off the dust of your feet" when they encountered people who did not receive them graciously.[34] Jesus loved people too much to let anything slow down the process of setting people free from their bondage whatever it is.

People who would rather be nice than Christian do not love enough. They do not have enough compassion. Instead, they are afraid of hurting someone or of being hurt. Remember, fear is the opposite of love. "Perfect love casts out all fear."[35]

If we really cared about people, we would not allow anyone to bully others into submission, instead we would want every person to feel free enough to express their hopes and dreams, to stretch their wings, and to reach their God-given potential. If we really loved people, we would not base our decisions on whether or not people would like us for those decisions. *Being nice or being liked is never a goal for followers of Jesus.*

What does being nice accomplish?

... more dysfunctional people
... fewer spiritual giants
... an intimidated congregation
... an inability to spread the Gospel
... little hope of renewal or growth
... discouraged church leaders

Being nice is not what Jesus wants from any of us.

One of the basic lessons I've learned as a consultant is that before renewal begins in a church or denomination, it is normal that someone has to leave or be denied. Almost every time a dying church attempts to thrive once again, someone tries to bully the leadership out of the attempt. And every time

---

[34] Matthew 10:14

[35] 1 John 4:18

there's a successful turnaround, people such as these are lost along the way because they are no longer allowed to get their way. When they can't get their way, they leave. Not even Jesus got through the journey with all of their disciples. Why should we expect too?

This does not mean that we should set out to intimate the bully or to kick people out of the church. But it *does* mean we care enough about the future of our church to not allow anyone to stifle its ability to liberate people from bondage or victimization. It means that we care enough about the bully that we will not allow the bully to intimidate the church because we know the spiritual vitality of both the bully and the church is at stake.

Matthew 18 gives us a formula for dealing with the dysfunctional bully. First, an individual privately confronts the person with what he/she is doing and asks the person to stop. If this doesn't achieve positive results, two or more people are to confront the person. If this does not resolve the matter, the person is to be brought before the entire church. Listen again to the not-so-nice words of Jesus. "*And if he shall neglect to hear them, tell it unto the church: but if he neglect to hear the church, let him be unto thee as a heathen man and a publican.*" In other words, withdraw from that person's presence, or in our case remove that person from office! Never, ever, allow such a person to dictate the direction of the church.[36]

The next time someone in your church attempts to intimidate or bully the church out of taking a positive step forward, go to God in prayer, and then get out the metal-tipped whip and drive that person out of the church ... of course in love.[37]

Bill Easum is founder of The Effective Church Group. a full-service church consulting and coaching group. You can reach him at easum@aol.com. You can visit his website at EffectiveChurch.com.

---

[36] Matthew 18:17

[37] For more on how to do this, see William M. Easum, *Sacred Cows Make Gourmet Burgers* (Nashville: Abingdon Press, 1995).

APPENDIX B

The Nuts and Bolts of Multi-Site

The simple definition of a Multi-Site church is "one church in many locations." In most cases this means one mission, same values, budget, staff, structure, etc.

When Dave Travis and Bill Easum wrote the book *Beyond The Box* in 2003 and included a chapter titled "Beyond a Single Location" the concept of Multi-Site was just beginning to gain some traction (by multisite we mean one church in multiple locations that shares the same staff, budget, and DNA). It was still debated by many whether it was a fad or tread. There were a few churches from which to extrapolate theory such as Community Christian Church in Naperville, North Pointe in Atlanta, First UMC Houston, North Coast in Vista, California, Evergreen Community church in the twin cities, but Multi-Site was in its infancy.

Later, when Bil Cornelius and I wrote *Go Big: Leading Your Church to Explosive Growth* in 2006, people were *still* debating trend or fad. There were a few more churches to draw information from such as LifeChurch.tv, Second Baptist Houston, Seacoast Church, and a few others, but having multiple campuses was not on very many pastor's minds. As churches began to expand into multiple campuses, trial and error became the only way to really learn how to do it. Often a church would start a second campus not out of strategy but because they were out of room and couldn't expand anymore where they were.

Today, the debate is over. Only an idiot would debate the wisdom and strategy of having multiple campuses to expand the kingdom. Now there is enough data to give solid advice on Multi-Site. This chapter is by no means the final authority on how to do multiple campuses, but it is the best of Bill Easum's wisdom.

In the beginning, most of the Multi-Site churches were trying to solve a problem. It was less a strategy than a way to continue their growth. Over time, these congregations realized the potential of Multi-Sites, and it developed into several forms of strategies.

The Untethered Church

We think of Multi-Site church as "untethered church" since they are not tied to a sacred place. The untethered church meets in many locations but has the same core values, mission, administration, budget, treasury, and the same staff. As such, they are reminiscent of the church of the first century that met in homes throughout the city but was considered the same church. Instead of relying on a location, the untethered church relies on mission and penetration into many corners of the city.

The theme that runs through all the examples we've seen is that property and space doesn't have to dictate the scope, nature, or quality of ministry. They are only tools that, if limited, requires innovative strategies. A heart for mission and conversion drives the Multi-Site congregation.

The key to understanding the Multi-Site movement is to remember that the mission of fulfilling the Great Commission is what drives these congregations rather than some philosophical understanding or strategy. It is not so much that these leaders set out to do Multi-Site ministry as it is being ready and open to the movement of God in one's life. In other words, to be able to grow when God says go.

Multi-Site should be seen as a vehicle to achieve a mission. They should never be the mission. If they quit working, you look for another way forward.

The primary reason Multi-Sites are so successful is because the additional sites draw on the successful DNA of a healthy church that is passionate about multiplying. Multi-Sites have the benefit of effective, proven staff, an established financial base, quality musicians and methods of discipleship from the beginning. It is best if Multi-Site leaders are home grown to pass on the DNA of the original church location. Multi-Site congregations build a "one church identity" through a variety of means, with the most common being sharing the same DNA, leadership structure, name, and teachers.

This method requires an intense commitment to a multiplication mindset. And the irony is the majority of the Multi-Site churches we track have also planted other churches. So we are not advocating an either/or; we are simply showing you how Multi-Sites absolutely leaves the door open to every option.

Reasons to Do Multisite

We know Multi-Site isn't for everyone, but we feel it is too great a strategy for any healthy church to dismiss without some major reflection and here are our reasons.

- Now that Multi-Sites have transitioned being an escape valve for an over crowed church to a growth strategy there is only one valid reason to open a second campus – because it meets people's needs and thus expands the kingdom.
- Some churches open a second site because they think it will cause growth. What we have learned is that *a second site doesn't cause a non-growing church to grow*. Only presently growing churches see their campuses thrive. So, if the reason you want to add another campus is because you think it will grow your church, you may see an initial bump, but generally the same reasons your church isn't growing in one campus will apply to two campuses too. If your church is meeting people's needs, then your church will grow no matter how many campuses you do, as long as you learn how to do them effectively.
- For some churches Multi-Sites are a church planting strategy. They see Multi-Sites as way to jump-start a plant that will eventually be separate units. Perimeter Church in Atlanta is an example.
- Multi-Sites are helpful in targeting a new age group (usually younger) or different psycho graphic groups. Mecklenburg Community Church is an example of this strategy.
- Another method is using Multi-Site to target a new geographical area with the same constituency the church has traditionally reached. Sometimes this is a newly developing suburban area and sometimes this is an in town neighborhood being populated by persons who have traditionally been reached by the church.
- Churches choose to start new campuses in friendlier confines because of opposition to building a new facility on the present campus due to space, area growth, governmental restrictions, and changing demographics.
- Multi-Sites are a great way to establish a new form of worship. In many cases there is a longstanding, center-city church with a traditional style that starts a new site with a contemporary style of worship at a new site.
- Multi-Sites allow a church to reach a new language or ethnicity different from the original congregation. Again, this is the same church, with the same leadership structure, but a new congregation on a new site that helps reach that language or ethnicity
- Multi-Sites can be used to help a struggling church regain its footing and start growing. A healthy church is asked by their judicatory to take a hurting church under their wing. In most cases, the healthy church takes a very strong leadership position over the hurting

congregation. The healthy church provides the staff and program for the hurting congregation.

- A growing number of Mainline churches are going Multiple-Site in order to get around the system. Usually this means the church retains the ability to choose the second site pastor rather than the system making the choice.

- One reason that can't be overstressed is that Multi-Site leaves all of the options open. In time the church can totally relocate. Many congregations in the 1960s bought too little land and have outgrown their property, or the neighborhood has changed so that the constituency no longer represents the area, or the facilities are so far out of date that it would cost more to repair and add on than to relocate, or the church needs to relocate, but the long-timers simply won't budge. The opening of a second, larger site gives the church the option decades later to totally move to the new site. This way, everyone wins.

- Multi-Sites have more open doors to new people than new congregations. Since the name of the church already has relationships within the community, some things are possible in a Multi-Site that might not be for a new church. Example: some schools require that churches using them have to purchase land or have plans to purchase land within a certain time. Utility companies require credit ratings for new churches. These rules don't apply to Multi-Sites.

- The laity is mobilized to a greater degree since going Multi-Site requires more leaders to be developed. It not only increases people's vision, it also forms a pipeline for the development of new leaders.

- Congregations are inspired to a greater vision which translates into more commitment to the original site and vision. The more locations the easier it is to see the ramifications of the Great Commission.

- Churches with limited land and a Great Commission mindset often find Multi-Site the most economical way to be faithful and grow.

- Often the number of dropouts from the original site who live near to the new site often re-engage with the church.

- Multi-Sites bring together the best of the large and small church.

Pitfalls To Avoid

Never underestimate the complexity of going Multi-Site. Multi-Site ministry is like a couple having their first child – everything changes and becomes more complex. However, once you've had one child, things get easier from there. The first Multi-Site is the toughest.

- Staff burnout is the number one pitfall to avoid. The following reduce burn out: regular coaching of the campus team, lay empowerment at the new campus, and staff who are addicted to new things.

- Not enough support for the campus pastor. By support we mean three things: financial backing in the beginning, regular involvement with the staff and Lead pastor; availability to all of the original campuses resources.

- Avoid using the terms "main campus" or "satellite campus." Doing so implies everything else is second-class.

- Trying to save a declining church. Your church must be healthy *before* starting.

- Thinking of the new site as an extra location rather than one church in many locations.

- Not spending the time, energy, and money needed.

Funding the New Campus

First, you should realize what it will cost you more if you don't find more room. If you're church isn't expanding, it will begin to decline. Losing momentum is never a good thing.

Here are some rules of thumb for funding:

- Most new sites cost between $50,000 and $150,000. Start-up costs vary greatly. $100,000 is a good figure to begin with and go upward.

- Most of the churches expect the new site to become self-supporting within one to two years maximum.

- Churches should expect to spend between 2–10 percent of their budget on a new site.

- Most (76 percent) of the churches take the money from the church budget without taking a special offering. Most keep the income streams centralized into one budget.

Staffing the New Site

Although this varies, plan on staffing the following: (1) a campus pastor; (2) someone to oversee the adult small groups; (3) worship leading; and (4) children's ministry. Each staff member should be in place and working the area before going public. Often, these folks come from within the existing staff of the primary location, ensuring good DNA.

In the beginning, the only full time person is the campus pastor. You should bring paid or unpaid staff on board with the view in mind of moving them to full time as soon as possible.

The Leadership Issue

The more sites you have, the more leadership opportunities you will have. Don't be afraid to do things that require more leaders. Don't avoid doing things that will require more leaders and celebrate that your need of leaders is growing. As you grow more leaders, you grow the sites. More jobs means more people in hands on ministry. The core staff must be more like athletic directors. They aren't just coaches or great athletes. They know how to oversee coaches who run teams. The best campus pastor is someone with a heart for developing leaders and who strives on mentoring apprentices. This person must have a heart for multiplication.

The most successful staff usually comes from within the congregation. Many are second career people. Eighty percent of Multi-Site churches develop leaders from within their small group system. If you don't have that in place before starting, you will have major leadership issues.

One of the keys to success is to constantly reinforce the DNA through regular contact with the campus pastor so that all of the campuses are aligned with the vision.

Here are several ways to immediately improve your campus strength.

1. Hire a better leader to run the campus. This is by far the best way to turn a campus around quickly. As goes the leader, so goes the campus.
2. Get a better lead singer for the band or remove someone who is "awkward" on stage. Pastors, send your spouse or top executive (or volunteer) over to your second site with a critical eye.
3. Give your worship space a makeover. Remove the drum shield and replace your drums with electric if the room is too small for live drums. Have you ever been to a major concert with a plexiglass drum shield? Didn't think so. Repaint the room, get nicer chairs, improve your lighting system, remove music stands from the stage, etc.
4. Remake your children's spaces to be very clean, inviting, and safe, and over staff them with people that look great, have all passed a background check, and do not look like they are the opening band for Marylin Manson. Mom's first impression must foster trust.
5. Make sure you have an attractive entrance with adequate parking. In most cases, if you can't park them you can't grow them.
6. Recruit greeters and parking attendants that are inviting and warm. Give your parking attendants maps to the property, umbrellas if it's raining, and walkie-talkies if your parking area is either large or divided.
7. Advertise after doing a massive remodel to the buildings, even if you are in a setup/breakdown situation.

When to Close a Campus

If you have multiple campuses and have never considered closing one, it's probably not a sign they are all good, but a sign that you are in denial. Here are a few critical reasons to close a campus.

- The campus is losing money. We can't over emphasize this one reason enough. Once a campus has had a year to eighteen months, they should be approaching a break-even point. If this is not happening, a change is needed or you may need to shut it down.
- Your first site is too thin to stay strong because the new campus site has sucked the life out of it by taking too many of your good people.
- When you realize that the costs necessary to make the site great and you are not willing to pay that price. It's only fair then, instead of stringing the people at that campus along, to promptly shut it down.

When closing a campus, we recommend doing it with as little fanfare as possible and being honest with the people. When you must close a campus, tell the truth and help the people either move to one of our other locations or transition to another local church.

If you think it's too scary to close a campus, then you should never enter the Multi-Site space because as you add campuses, no matter how successful you are, eventually the odds are you will have to close one.

Self-Supporting Within Eighteen Months

Every campus should be working to pay their bills by the end of twelve to eighteen months. If a campus is not paying their bills by this time, you making one of the following errors: you are over-paying for a lease or mortgage; over paying staff salaries; or you aren't drawing enough people. We have found that a campus needs to average over 250 to be self-supporting and/or have the building paid off (no mortgage or lease payment).

If you are renting space by the weekend or hour, meaning you are in a setup/tear down situation, be prepared to burn your people out more quickly. Either you need to hire someone who specializes in this particular area, or you are going to need to move your church into something more permanent within a few years.

Are You Ready To Go Multi-Site?

The following are the questions Bill Easum asks when consulting with churches considering going Multi-Site.

- Is my church growing each of the last five years by at least 5 percent?
- Is my primary worship hour at least 80 percent full?

- Is my church experiencing any kind of outside interference from the community?
- Is my church well respected in the community?
- Is the leadership comfortable with releasing present members to form the core of the new site?
- Are we trying to reach more people, different people, or impact a new area of town or the country?
- Do my leaders understand and covet the ministry of multiplication?
- Can we add this new location without financially damaging the original campus?
- Do we have the money to fund the site for two years?
- Do we have a capable person to send out to be the campus pastor?
- Do we thoroughly understand and appreciate the demographics of the new area?
- Are we organizationally competent enough to take on this complication ministry?

If you answered "Yes" to all the above you are ready to go Multi-Site.

Conclusion

The primary reason Multi-Sites are so successful is because the additional sites draw on the successful DNA of a healthy church that is passionate about multiplying. Multi-Sites have the benefit of effective, proven staff, an established financial base, quality musicians and methods of discipleship from the beginning. It is best if Multi-Site leaders are home grown to pass on the DNA of the original church location. Multi-Site congregations build a "one church identity" through a variety of means, with the most common being sharing the same DNA, leadership structure, name, and teachers.

ABOUT THE AUTHORS

Bill Easum has a thirty-year track record of growing congregations in two denominations. His last church, which he re-started and pastored for twenty-four years, grew to be one of the largest United Methodist Churches in South Texas. Since 1987 Bill has devoted his time to consulting, coaching, and speaker. Bill is the Founder and President of The Effective Church Group.

The years have been good to Bill. He's had the privilege of helping over 700 churches grow around the world, authored twenty-one books, received the prestigious Donald McGavran award for outstanding church leadership, and had a wife who was strong enough to hold him accountable. These days Bill spends his time coaching leaders because helping churches grow is still his life's passion.

Bill is a graduate of Baylor University, B.A., Southwestern Baptist Theological Seminary, M.D., and Perkins School of Theology, S.T.M.

Bill is a widower and has one daughter, Caran.

You can reach Bill at Easum@aol.com

Bill Tenny-Brittian is an author, speaker, coach, and consultant on all things church growth. Ordained in the Christian Church (Disciples of Christ), he has served as both a church planter and a church transformational change agent in churches literally from coast to coast. He is a regular contributor to *Net Results* magazine, adjunct professor for Pastoral Leadership and for Evangelism at Phillips Seminary, and the managing partner of The Effective Church Group.

This is the tenth book Bill has had a hand in. His other books include *Big Mouse: The Fine Art of Herding Cats; Prayer for People Who Can't Sit Still; Hitchhikers' Guide to Evangelism; High-Voltage Spirituality;* and *Effective Staffing for Vital Churches.*

Bill is a popular speaker and workshop presenter and has been leading workshops at the Exponential East Conference for several years on discipleship and church growth.

Bill holds a BTh from Florida Baptist College with a specialization in New Testament and Church Planting; an MDiv from Candler School of Theology, Emory University with a specialization in Old Testament Studies; and a DMin in Church Multiplication Movements from Northwest Graduate School in Seattle.

He is married to Dr. Kris Tenny-Brittian and together they reside in Columbia, Missouri.

You can reach Bill at billtb@EffectiveChurch.com.

Made in the USA
San Bernardino, CA
22 June 2018